Elizabeth S

How to pass examina

G000141602

ECONOMICS

Bryan Richards, B.A. (Econ.)

Head of Economics, Rugby School
Chief Examiner to AEB (O Level) and SREB
(CSE) Assistant Examiner at A Level

Cassell · London

CASSELL LTD.
1 St. Anne's Road, Eastbourne, East Sussex BN21 3UN

© T. B. Richards 1979

First published 1979
Second impression 1981
Third impression 1983

ISBN 0 304 30284 8

Text set in 10/11 pt Photon Times, printed and bound
in Great Britain by Richard Clay (The Chaucer Press) Ltd,
Bungay, Suffolk

General introduction

The aim of this series is to provide tutorial books that will help students pass their examinations by showing them how to tackle problems in a subject. They spotlight the essential concepts in a subject and deal with those aspects that give most trouble to students. They provide not only the answers, but, where necessary, the reasoning behind them. More important, they point the way to the solution of similar problems.

It is assumed that the student will also possess a standard textbook for background information and further reflection and practice.

The books should be useful both to the private student working on his own, with or without a correspondence course, and to the college student, for use in class and for private revision. Every subject has its special language, its approach to problems, its mode of thought. By studying a book which highlights the essentials, the student will quickly learn to master the examination techniques required by the subject.

The authors do not set out to give 'model' or perfect answers to descriptive questions, nor to explore every possible aspect of a question. To do so would be impossible within the time-limits imposed by an examination. The aim has been to provide the sort of answer examiners look for but rarely find: the answer in which the essential points are stressed and the irrelevant, or even in some cases, subsidiary points are omitted.

The commentaries and notes that go with the questions should be carefully studied. If the student does not understand them, he should go back and cover the relevant section of the syllabus again. At a later stage it may be helpful to attempt the questions himself and compare the result with the original answer. During the pre-examination revision period, questions should be practised within the time-limits allowed in the examination. In this way self-confidence can be built up and the technique assimilated. Reading a book, although helpful, is not enough; to succeed, hard work and constant practice are required.

In the examination room

1. Relax. Take a few deep breaths.
2. Read the examination paper through twice. Pay particular attention to the instructions: how many questions you have to answer, and which are compulsory.

3. Decide how much time you can afford to give to each question, including time at the end for quick revision.
4. If there is a choice of questions, select those you intend to answer.
5. Unless instructed otherwise, you do not have to answer questions in the order set. Choose the easiest question and do that first. *But* always answer any compulsory questions early on.
6. Answer all the questions asked for. If you run short of time, give a skeleton answer rather than no answer at all: remember that no answer means no marks.

These are the points to observe in planning the writing of the paper as a whole. There are however some points to bear in mind while answering each question:

1. Read the question carefully and decide exactly what the examiner requires you to do. Ask yourself why he has set the question in those words. Be sure you answer the question that has been set.
2. Plan your answer. Make brief notes of the points you must cover on scrap paper before you begin. Further ideas may occur to you as you write, but you should have a clear idea of the general structure of the answer beforehand.
3. Write concisely. Keep to the point: a good, short answer will score far more marks than a long, rambling one. Padding wastes valuable time and fools no one.
4. Write legibly and neatly. This is particularly important in figure work. The examiner cannot give you credit for work if he cannot read it.

Preface

Examining candidates in the subject of Economics has undergone drastic changes in recent years, to such an extent that there are now three distinct methods by which this exercise can be achieved:

a. the essay test;
b. the objective test;
c. the data response or stimulus material test.

All three methods give varying degrees of satisfaction to both candidate and examiner, and the general consensus of opinion is that some combination of these papers will offer the most worthwhile means of assessment.

It is well known that multiple choice testing counteracts the tendency towards candidates' being 'crammed' and taught to reproduce standard or model essay answers: it thereby provides a more effective platform for economic understanding. But the essay question technique still has a very important part to play in allowing candidates to analyse problems, express arguments and confirm those arguments by the methodical sifting and presentation of relevant evidence.

Any author intending to produce 'model essay answers' to examination questions is treading a dangerous tightrope, and I am well aware that my attempt to provide 'specimen' answers will not meet with everyone's approval. They should be regarded as suggested guidelines for those candidates who find it difficult to assess what may be required by examining bodies. There is certainly no implication that there is only one way to produce a particular essay answer, but I hope that the material included, and the degree of emphasis placed on certain points within the essays, will give candidates an awareness of the depth and relevance required.

Perhaps the most difficult problem encountered in completing this book was keeping to a realistic length of specimen answer. *There is no doubt that some of the answers are too long and the average candidate would be hard pressed to produce similar essays in the time allowed. The object of the exercise is not one of full-scale imitation, but for the salient points to emerge in an essay context.* These key ideas are included more specifically in the 'comments' section and form an indispensable part of the theme of the question.

This book, then, is intended to meet the needs of those students taking the advanced level economics examination in any of the GCE Boards, along with those students taking economics as part of their professional examinations in subjects such as accountancy, banking and commerce. The book is seen as a complementary aid to an existing study of a conventional textbook in economics, the main purpose being to highlight certain key areas of the syllabus (there is no intention of covering an entire syllabus), and investigate the area thoroughly.

The format adopted is as follows:

1. Introductory chapters:
   a. an economist's functions;
   b. an economist's techniques;
   c. an economist's preparation for examinations.

2. The selection of a number of key areas of study, most of which could be assumed as forming a common core in many of the economics examinations encountered.

3. The production of a specimen answer to a typical essay question within the confines of the particular study area.

4. Specific and general comments are made on the answers, so that candidates are guided to the main relevant points; their attention is drawn to the correct balance between the arguments; and suggestions are made as to the correct presentation of ideas and their illustration by diagrams. Common sources of confusion as well as detailed explanation and illustration of many peripheral issues are included.

5. Finally, similar essay titles on the topic area with suggestions for further reading from appropriate text books provide an all-embracing analysis.

The following examination bodies have given permission to reproduce questions set by them in previous examinations for which the author is extremely grateful:

AEB	Associated Examining Board for the General Certificate of Education
JMB	Joint Matriculation Board
Oxf.	Oxford Delegacy of Local Examinations
O/C Board	Oxford and Cambridge Schools Examination Board
SU	Southern Universities Joint Board for School Examinations
Camb.	University of Cambridge Local Examinations Syndicate
Lond	University of London University Entrance and School Examination Council
WJEC	Welsh Joint Education Committee
IB	Institute of Bankers
ICWA	Institute of Chartered Acccountants
CA	Certified Accountants

Mr L. B. Curzon, Principal of the London College for the Distributive Trades, and a former chief examiner in Economics, has been very helpful in reading the typescript and offering many valuable comments. I am deeply indebted to him, as I am to Mr E. Baker, a former HMI and the chief motivator of this series. I would also like to place on record the help I received from Dr Philip Stevens, one of my teaching colleagues, whose mathematical advice has proved invaluable. My departmental colleague, Dr David Richardson has given me some sound advice, enabling me to simplify the text and improve the original draft.

Finally, my deepest gratitude goes to my wife for being so patient and tactful during the writing of this book. Her ability to occupy the attention of our children, while at the same time managing to make the odd searching comment, enabled me to continue unhindered in the final stages of the book.

T.B.R.

Contents

What does an economist actually do?

Introduction

The layman can certainly answer that question—'an economist studies economic problems but can't solve them'. The ordinary man in the street would like to know why the cost of living is always rising so rapidly; why there are so many strikes in British industry; why the government appears unable to halt the rise in unemployment; and why our livelihood is often affected by changes in the rate of exchange. It does seem ludicrous that an advanced society can send a man to the moon—and bring him back safely—and yet find it impossible to isolate the true causes of inflation.

Perhaps economists are not doing their job properly. What is their job? It was Keynes who said that the task of the economist was to utilise the technique of thinking—'the theory of Economics is a method rather than a doctrine, an apparatus of the mind, a technique of thinking which helps its possessor to draw correct conclusions' (J. M. Keynes). The economist is a thinking animal, who according to Professor Lipsey must avoid the temptation to memorise as 'memorisation is the royal road to disaster in economics' (R. Lipsey). But what is it they should be thinking about?

Content

The answer to the question posed above lies in the multitude of interpretations of the subject matter of economics.

a. 'The nature of economic analysis ... consists of deductions from a series of postulates, the chief of which are almost universal facts of experience' (Lord Robbins).
b. 'Political Economy, or Economics, is a study of mankind in the ordinary business of life; it examines that part of individual and social action which is most closely connected with the attainment and with the use of the material requisites of well being' (Professor A. Marshall).
c. 'Economics is an inquiry into the nature and causes of the Wealth of Nations' (Adam Smith).
d. 'Economics is a social science studying how people attempt to accommodate scarcity to their wants and how these attempts interact through exchange' (A. Cairncross).

Probably the most generally acceptable definition of the subject is that it is 'the science which studies human behaviour as a relationship between ends and scarce means which have alternative uses' (Lionel Robbins). We can say quite simply that the task of the economist is to study the alternative ways and means by which it is possible to allocate resources in society, and to evaluate the implications of using resources in one way rather than another. In short he studies the working of the economic system and puts economic activity under the microscope.

Economic activity

Firms respond to the demands placed upon them by purchasing relatively scarce resources which finally culminate in the production of an assortment of different goods and services. The demand for goods and services by the consumers is supplemented by the demand in the factor market for raw materials, labour etc., from the entrepreneurs. Costs are being incurred when these resources are bought but the mirror image of these costs are the incomes of the work force, which are likely to be respent, thereby maintaining the circular flow of income. The productive impetus of the economy is being refuelled. The study of economic activity has no beginning and no end, but is a circular and interdependent mechanism which is self-generated.

The production of goods and services gives consumers direct satisfaction or helps firms to enlarge their capacity, and it can be said that the contribution of the government to the creation of the Gross National Product is becoming frighteningly large. The private sector is being squeezed with detrimental effects on the freedom and variety of choice of consumer goods. One could argue the seemingly rapacious appetite of the State for the scarce resources is caused by the inability of the private sector to supply sufficient quantities of certain goods and services, e.g. defence, education and social services. The State produces goods and services which are capable of being sold to the public (coal, electricity) along with items which appear to be given away for nothing (health, parks, road networks).

The common axiom 'you can't get something for nothing' is never better illustrated than by the fact that the State finances itself by resorting to taxing the public or borrowing from the public. Further finance has to be obtained if necessary from the banking system, with severe repercussions on the inflationary state of affairs.

The ceiling up to which an economy can produce is determined by the full and efficient utilisation of the combination of factors of production available to that economy, and society will have to allocate the resources to their different uses.

Resource allocation and the opportunity cost involved lie at the heart of the basic economic problem facing all economies, and the economist must play his part in helping to analyse the different facets of the problem.

The economist's method

All economic problems are really the same problem set in different contexts, that is, how people behave in allocating scarce resources among competing uses. The need to 'economise' results in the study of economics.

The economist is an analyst but *human behaviour* is exceedingly difficult to analyse scientifically. The scientist may be able to isolate the substances in which he is interested, but the economist's raw material is the human species: not only will one person differ from another in his or her reactions but even the same person will react differently at times to the same circumstances. Man is subjected to emotional pressures which outweigh the rational ideas with which man is supposed to be blessed. A person who disapproves of jewellery may refuse to hold shares in a gold mine—hardly the act of a rational man. Human behaviour is erratic and cannot be predicted precisely. The economist's laboratory is the real world where extraneous influences cannot be syphoned off and held in abeyance. They have to be assumed to remain constant.

The economist does not decide on the *ends* to which scarce resources are devoted. That role can be allowed to rest on the shoulders of society, ably supported by the government. The economist's job is to analyse, interpret and offer the likely implications of varying actions carried out by companies, individuals and governments. Society may strive to achieve as fast a rate of growth as possible, and the economist can help by investigating the possible avenues to achieve faster growth, along with the consequences to society of going in a particular direction. The objectivity of the economist gives rise to the concept of 'positive' rather than 'normative' analysis, in that he sees his task as analysing something which can be verified by an appeal to empirical knowledge. It is not for him to consider the merits of a country being on a fixed- or floating-exchange-rate system, but to consider the economic consequences of allowing the rate to depreciate. Of course, he has his own personal viewpoints—he would be very dull indeed without them—but he must try to suppress his own preferences in the interests of a completely objective approach which can be confirmed by the facts.

The economist finds himself in a situation where he is establishing a set of principles or theories about the way in which the economic system functions. He is faced by a very complex world with terribly complicated interrelationships. Mere observation of these events will not help to clarify and confirm the economist's beliefs as to the causation of some of these actions. The construction of *models* occurs so that parts of the whole economy can be investigated in the hope of reaching a solution to specific problems.

The search for a methodological approach which is scientific in nature would require the following steps:

1. *The selection of the problem to be studied.* This can range from something like 'what are the main determinants of the rate of infla-

tion in the United Kingdom?' to a problem such as 'What are the economic consequences of building a Channel Tunnel?"

2. *The definition of the terms and concepts incorporated in the model.* All the variables must be measurable, so that any changes in them can be quantified. The language of the economist can cause confusion among the laymen, as economics has a jargon of its own. What exactly does 'money' mean? What is 'investment'?

3. *A set of assumptions.* To simplify the investigation, assumptions are made which tend to ignore or abstract from those determinants thought to be of minor importance. Emphasis can then be paid to those variables regarded as major influences. There are assumptions obviously regarded as extremely hypothetical such as a world of only two countries producing only two goods A and B. But many other assumptions have the backing of generalised tendencies of the economy at large, such as firms attempting to maximise their profits, and consumers trying to maximise their satisfaction obtained from their purchases.

4. *Deductive reasoning must take place.* Logical deductions can be formulated based on the assumptions, and if we assume all influences other than interest rates to be unimportant in determining investment expenditure, it follows that entrepreneurs' investment plans will be affected by the rate of interest.

5. *Predictions can now be offered.* These represent a hypothesis which should be reliable. The idea that consumption is dependent upon income is thought to be reliable enough upon which to base predictions with some degree of certainty. The relationship between the money supply and the level of activity within a country forms the basis of yet another prediction which states that the growth in the supply of money will result in a rise in the price level—but after an interval of twelve to eighteen months.

6. *The theory must be tested by reference to the facts.* Simple models do not attempt to describe the real world; they exist to analyse the major forces operating in a realistic situation. A great number of items are abstracted from the model to allow for a closer study of one or two of the key features. However the model can become extremely complex when it attempts to include all the many variables capable of influencing an event. But are these models really useful? Can they be used to predict the consequences of certain actions? Evidence must be considered and statistical data analysed before a theory can be accepted or disproved. Many convincing theories of their time have been successfully challenged by circumstances, and finally replaced by more up to date theories. Such an occasion must have occurred in 1936 when Keynes' *General Theory* was published, which incorporated a set of ideas which challenged the unchallengeable classical economists of the 1930s. A theory is only as successful as the facts which support the conclusions offered. Is the theory useful in explaining or predicting behaviour in the real world?

Conclusion

A student of economics must have the capacity to understand the principles upon which an economy works and be able to apply those principles to the particular problem in hand. A deductive or an inductive approach can be adopted, with the latter looking at facts first and then introducing a theory designed to fit those facts. This capacity to handle, interpret and present statistical evidence upon which economic decisions are reached, should have a high priority in the economist's armoury of weapons. Keynes however saw the role of the economist somewhat differently:

'The study of economics does not seem to require any specialised gifts of an unusually high order. Is it not, intellectually regarded, a very easy subject compared with the higher branches of philosophy or pure science? An easy subject at which very few excel! The paradox finds its explanation, perhaps in that the master-economist must possess a rare combination of gifts. He must be a mathematician, historian, statesman, philosopher—in some degree. He must understand symbols and speak in words. He must contemplate the particular in terms of the general and touch abstract and concrete in the same flight of thought. He must study the present in the light of the past for the purposes of the future. No part of man's nature or his institutions must lie entirely outside his regard. He must be purposeful and disinterested in a simultaneous mood; as aloof and incorruptible as an artist, yet sometimes as near the earth as a politician'.   (J. M. Keynes)

The techniques used by economists

Why do economists need models?

The sole purpose of a model is to simplify complex relationships so that a clear understanding can emerge. Models are there to be observed; they do not have to be an exact replica of the real thing. Often only major features of a behavioural pattern are included. A close study of these models will enable predictions to be made when the model is activated, and a useful test of such a model is to compare the predictions with the actual occurrences in the real world.

Economists must be careful not to oversimplify in the construction of their model, and must aim to incorporate assumptions which are as realistic as possible. A model is built then to attempt to solve a problem—which may be anything from 'what affects the demand for motor cars?' to investigating the 'main reasons for the level of the circular flow of income'.

The problem in question can be labelled *the dependent variable*, while the model would also contain *independent variables*. Any changes in these independent variables would certainly affect the behaviour of the dependent variable, but also would affect the independent variables themselves. It can be said that the variables are *interdependent*. It is extremely difficult to quantify the specific influence of *one* independent variable (price of motor cars) on a dependent variable (demand for motor cars), especially when it is obvious that other factors (incomes, government policy, tastes) are in the background and are changing.

The economist's solution is to accept these important variables within the model, but hold them constant, while the influence of a specific independent variable is being considered. This device is commonly called *ceteris paribus* or 'other things remaining equal'.

How are these relationships best illustrated?

Economics abounds with relationships between two or more variables, and most textbooks express them in one or all of the following ways:

1. *In Words*: it probably takes longer to say what you mean especially when the subject has a jargon of its own. Precise thinking entails the precise meaning of the words used. Most schoolteachers would ap-

preciate the difficulty caused by the use of the terms 'saving' and 'investment'.

2. *In Mathematics*: verbal statements can be shortened to good effect by the use of symbols allied to numbers. The seemingly complex statement that 'the multiplier is the ratio of the change in income to the permanent change in the flow of expenditure that brought it about' can be shortened to the simple algebraic statement:

$$K = \frac{\Delta Y}{\Delta J}$$ (K = the multiplier

Y = change in income

J = change in injections).

Variables which are dependent upon each other can be given symbols, and the relationship can be expressed in the following terms:

$X = f(A)$ (X = demand for meat
A = price of meat
f = depends upon).

3. *In Graphical Form*: this is the nearest medium to a picture form, and is possibly the most widely used method in economics when it comes to representing the dependence of one variable upon another. It can be allied to the geographer's dependence upon map work, and therefore it would repay candidates handsomely in understanding, if time were spent on analysing the construction and interpretation of graphs—not forgetting the many pitfalls the unwary traveller may stumble across.

Essential requirements in the construction of a correctly drawn graph

1. *The Axes*: candidates must first draw vertical and horizontal lines, intersecting at an angle of 90 degrees, at a point called the origin (O). The vertical line is often called the y axis, and the horizontal line is called the x axis. (See diagram no. 1 overleaf.)

2. *Positive and Negative values*: the x and y axes are divided up into separate units called a scale, which illustrates both positive and negative values. Positive values of x are measured to the right of the origin, and negative values of x to the left. Above the origin there are positive values of y and below the origin the y values become negative. Economic textbooks tend to concentrate on relationships of variables within the North-East quadrant (shaded area) which contain the positive values of both x and y.

3. *The Coordinates*: before a graph can be drawn separate points have to be plotted. A point is obtained by specifying values of x and y, thereby producing the coordinates for that point. It is usual to quote the x value first, followed by the y value.
   e.g. $A = (3, 4)$

4. *The Scale*: both axes are divided into units, each of which is represented

by a specific number of centimetres. But it is important to remember that the scale on each axis may be independent of the other.

5. *The Labels*: each axis must be clearly and accurately labelled to indicate the nature and value of the appropriate variables. In economics, convention rules that the price or cost variable be placed on the *y* axis, while any time variable is placed along the *x* axis. Quantities demanded or supplied, which are usually placed on the *x* axis, must contain the time element, whether it be per day, per week or even per year.

6. *The Complete Graph*: the related values of *x* and *y* can be plotted as points, which, when joined up, allows a line or curve to emerge. Care must be taken to remember to label this line.

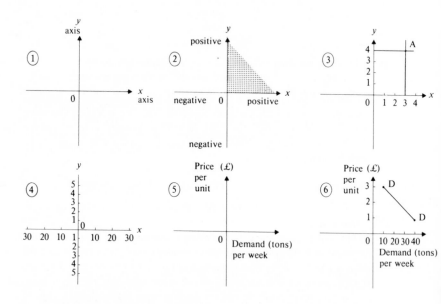

The significance of the curve on the graph

Lines are drawn on a graph to represent the way in which one variable is a function of the other. The lines are normally referred to as curves and they fall into two main categories: linear curves (straight lines) and non-linear curves (non-straight lines).

The two most important features of a curve are its direction on the graph and its slope.

Direction

A downward sloping line to the right always describes an 'inverse' relationship between the variables involved. Actual numbers of units on the axes, although important, are secondary to the overriding significance of a negative change in one variable being accompanied by a positive change in the other variable. It is useful to think of a reduction in one of the variables as a 'negative increase'. This relationship is illustrated in Fig. 1, when a price reduction is associated with an increase in the quantity demanded.

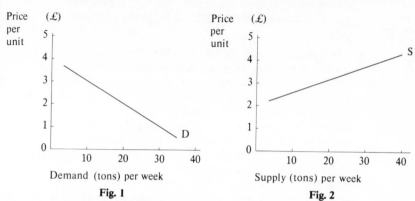

Fig. 1　　　　　　　　　Fig. 2

An upward sloping line to the right will always describe a 'positive' relationship between the variables involved. The line in Fig. 2 illustrates the fact that as price rises (or falls), so will the quantity supplied rise (or fall). Sometimes this principle is illustrated by saying that supply is an increasing function of price.

Slope of a linear curve

1. *Measurement*

The slope of a linear curve can be easily understood and measured if it is compared with the gradient of a hill. A runner would prefer to run up a hill which is 1 in 10, rather than one which is 1 in 2. This means that for every 10 yards travelled in a horizontal direction the road only rises by 1 yard: any runner would prefer to run up the first slope rather than to have to combat a hill which is really steep. Slope is nothing more than measuring the change in one variable as a result of a change in another. It is the ratio of the distance moved up the y axis to the distance moved along the x axis, and is frequently seen as a fraction such as $\frac{1}{2}$ or $\frac{1}{4}$. The slope of the curve in Fig. 3 would be 1 in 5 or AC/CB, with the greater the fraction, the greater the slope of the curve. It will also be seen that every straight line curve has the same slope at every point, that is, a constant slope.

2. *Value: negative/positive*

The slope of a linear curve is a measure of how one variable changes in relation to another, and the higher its value the steeper the slope. But a slope may be regarded as 'negative' if it is downward sloping to the right,

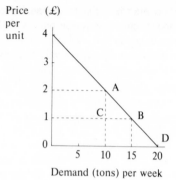

Fig. 3

in that it shows an inverse relationship between the two variables. For instance, a reduction in price from £2 to £1 (a negative increase of £1) is related to an increase in the quantity demanded from 20 to 30 tons (a positive increase of 10 tons) i.e. $-1/+10$ which is finally a negative value. This can be illustrated by the downward sloping demand curve in Fig. 4.

There are other linear curves which have the same slope as the one above, but the value is regarded as 'positive'. Linear curves which are upward sloping to the right exhibit the principle of a positive relationship between the two variables involved. The supply curve in Fig. 5 shows that

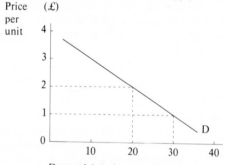

Fig. 4

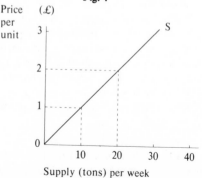

Fig. 5

a rise (or fall) in price is related to an increase (or decrease) in the quantity supplied. The ratio for the two variables in this case is always 1:10 and can be shown as a fraction $+1/+10$ (or $-1/-10$ for a fall in price and quantity). In either case the answer will be positive.

Slope of a non-linear curve:

A non-linear curve will possess a slope which is continually changing, and measurement of such a slope causes more problems. ABCDE are points placed on the curve in Fig. 6. The slope of the curve from B to E might be measured by the vertical distance EF over the horizontal distance BF, but this would falsify the answer as all that is being done is measuring the slope of the straight line BE, and not the curve between these points. To attempt to measure the curve between B and D will give yet a different answer, indicating a steeper slope.

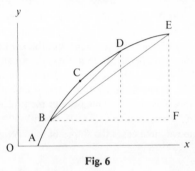

Fig. 6

Trying to calculate the slope of a curve at a particular point (see Fig. 7) involves the use of tangents being drawn at the point itself. Once the tangent is drawn at point B, the slope of that line can be worked out by conventional means, with the realisation that the slope of a straight line has a constant value. If tangents were drawn at different points on the curve, one can quickly see that the slope of the curve at these points is not constant. For example, the slope at B is equal to BG/HG, while the slope at E is different, JK/EK.

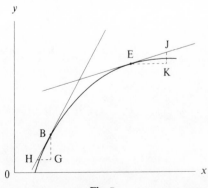

Fig. 7

Assuming HG and EK are similar unit increases in X, it is obvious that BG is greater than JK and would give a much larger fraction as the slope.

One major source of confusion

Which graph line (Figs. 8–10) has the greatest slope?

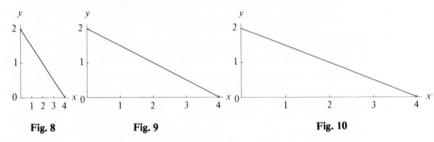

Fig. 8   Fig. 9   Fig. 10

In fact they all have the same slope, but the apparent steepness of the line in Fig. 8 gives the impression that it has the greatest slope. The key factor is the scale employed for the graphs. The use of different scales along the horizontal X axes will necessitate lines of different steepness, but not of different slopes, as slope is a measure of the rate at which Y exchanges for a unit of X.

In the above three cases the slopes of the lines are all in the ratio of 1 to 2.

Examination preparation

The study of economics is regarded as a science, but the preparation for an examination in economics (or any other subject for that matter) is undoubtedly an art. A mastery of examination technique must be seen as a vital piece of equipment in the armoury of the economist examinee, as without it, he (or she) may not be able to convince the examiner that the subject matter is completely understood. An examination tries to achieve many things ranging from obtaining a creative response to certain questions, to allowing candidates develop both sides of an argument followed by a conclusion. The successful candidate will be able to display a knowledge of economic concepts and an ability to analyse problems applying fundamental principles to questions of policy.

Prior to Examination

1. *Obtain the official syllabus* from the board or body to which the examination is connected. Check on the type of examination question likely to occur within the particular paper to be studied. A familiarity with typical examination papers will give candidates the confidence sound answers require. Most Boards give notification of a change of syllabus some two years in advance, and specimen questions may be forwarded on application.

2. *Cover all the syllabus*—or at least as much of the syllabus as is possible—within the time constraints under which candidates find themselves. Although a judicious selection of topics, on which to concentrate, can bring success, there is a grave danger that 'putting all your eggs in one basket' can cause problems on the day of the examination. Syllabus coverage is even more essential in an economics examination, especially when that examination contains an objective test.

3. *Know your subject thoroughly*—there is no substitute for a comprehensive coverage and complete appreciation of the topics involved. Even seemingly ambiguous questions become plainly transparent in the light of a sound understanding of the subject matter. There's a lot of truth in the statement that one can only understand an economics course completely when one has covered the course fully. A topic is only appreciated when other topics are related to it.

4. *Revise and practise essay writing*—the vast quantity of material contained in any course must be modified for easy revision, and index cards on certain topics can easily be produced to give assistance at a period when time is an invaluable commodity. But even the tremendous boost an assortment of index cards can give, would be of little avail without putting into practice the essay writing exercise an examination demands. Practice makes perfect in many walks of life and essay writing is no exception. Most examinations of the standard being studied here contain papers of two and a half to three hours, with approximately four essays being expected within that time period. Getting used to settling down in a desk for three hours and apportioning time between essays can only be simulated by actually doing it. Familiarity in this case does not breed contempt, but conquers nervousness.

In the examination room

1. Make sure you have all *the necessary equipment*. It may seem obvious that a pen must be brought to the examination, but a spare pen, pencil, ruler and rubber will be useful additions to the well-equipped candidate. Many examination rooms contain a clock, but it is always advisable to have your own watch—in case of accidents. A calculator can also be used to advantage—if it is allowed for specialist work.

2. *Read the question paper—thoroughly*. The instructions on the examination paper are there for a purpose, and must be read carefully. There are still some candidates who do not scrutinise the rubric, and the inclusion of different sections to the paper can cause unforseen difficulties. Even advanced level candidates have been known to ignore the reverse side of an examination paper, by which action, a small number of questions have remained undiscovered.

3. *Select the essays to be answered*. Having compared the level of difficulty between the essays—as far as the candidate is concerned—a selection must be made. This selection need not necessarily be strictly adhered to, as within the examination time-span, the examinee's original choices might alter. The candidate's interests will be best served if the order in which the essays are attempted is geared to an ascending condition of difficulty. While an equal amount of time should be spent on each essay, it is understandable that candidates would want to allow more time for those essays they consider well within their grasp. Even so, it would be foolish to misallocate their available time to such an extent that the last essay becomes a non-starter. It is useful to jot down a list of times when the various questions should be finished. One can then see at a glance the time which has to be made up. However in the event of a misallocation of time candidates should complete the answer in note form, or in such a way as to convince the examiner of the main points intended.

4. *Plan the essays.* Some candidates feel that they are so well equipped intellectually that they can plan their essay as they are in the process of writing it. These students are very few and far between, and even they might have attacked the essay in a more mature way if they had only seen fit to spend a few more minutes in thinking about and writing out a brief plan. The briefest of points are required for this, and with a skeleton to work from, the essay can be written with additional points being included at appropriate intervals.

The examination itself

1. *Essay writing generally*—Whatever the subject undertaken, candidates must search for a style and expression which will produce a clarity of thought best suited to an essay technique. Although the maxim 'quality before quantity' still holds, candidates must be prepared to think carefully and write quickly, if a fully developed answer is going to emerge. A clear grammatical construction, suitably punctuated and accurately spelt, must give candidates a favourable foundation for the subject matter contained in their work. The examiner's task is not an easy one and candidates must strive to facilitate their work by writing legibly. It is no use including a brilliant exposition of an economic argument if it cannot be read. Your script is one of many the examiner will mark—make sure he finds it a pleasure to read.

2. *Relevance required.* Not even a well organised and clearly presented paper stands much chance of success if the material contained in the answer is irrelevant. The logically formulated answer must include points strictly related to the question as set. It is most uneconomic to include material which will earn no marks and cost a great deal of a scarce resource—time! But candidates are renowned for answering the question they would like to see set! Relevance must be associated with balance, and with questions often including specific parts, every effort must be made to avoid the temptation to overemphasise the section which is well known to the detriment of sections which after all contain a certain proportion of marks.

3. *The actual question*
   a. The age old cry 'how do I begin?' can be simply accommodated by the candidate identifying that branch of economics which the examiner is trying to test. In some cases, it is painfully obvious that a particular area of economic theory is being investigated, but some questions can be seen as difficult starting points. A definite framework is required in most cases, and the model created by the candidate can be introduced by a simple explanatory statement, containing some clear definitions of the more important terms, in readiness for the more complex relationships which follow.
   b. The format of any answer must indicate a beginning, a middle and a conclusion, but even more vital is the balance between the key

items involved. No one wants to read an answer which disappears into thin air or is suspended in space, and likewise the development of the chosen points must bear a firm relationship with the significance of those points in the context of the essay chosen. This is one of the most difficult and perhaps, dangerous elements in essay writing, in that a candidate is liable to go completely astray in his choice of emphasised points.

c. Diagrams can assist in the clarity which candidates must be striving to achieve. But if they are going to be used in scripts, then they must be well drawn, accurately labelled and most importantly they must be explained within the context of the essay. Mere inclusion of an accurately drawn diagram means nothing, other than the fact that someone has memorised what could be a complicated series of lines imposed on a graph. It is wise to add that diagrams should be drawn in pencil as mistakes can easily be rectified with an eraser.

Some 'do nots'

1. *Do not* concentrate on just a few topics, hoping for a miracle.
2. *Do not* place complete reliance on last year's examination questions as a guide to what might not occur.
3. *Do not write more essays than asked for.*
4. *Do not* memorise answers—not even the ones that follow in this book—but use the information to enable you to apply the correct principles to particular questions.
5. *Do not* rely on this book as the answer to all your prayers. It must be regarded as complementing an established economics text book.

An important 'do'.

Do be professional concerning the examination. It signifies the end product of, in some cases, two years of hard work. In many ways it is unreal as it represents an opportunity—in anything from two and a half to three hours—to show how basic knowledge acquired over a long period of time can be used to tackle fresh problems. The examiner is not your opponent; he is merely there to judge that you have reached the standard set by the Board controlling the examination. Help the examiner to help you by adopting a realistic and professional approach, which will indicate that you have the capacity of logical thought, and powers of deduction and exposition.

Essay number 1

How does the market mechanism help to resolve the fundamental economic problem? What difficulties, if any, might arise were all activities to be determined by this mechanism alone? (O/C Board)

Suggested answer

Different economies have one thing in common—they all find that they have insufficient resources to satisfy the never ending demands of society. These scarce resources, and therefore the goods made from them, are capable of alternative uses involving society with a choice between alternatives. The decisions finally taken dictate not only the satisfaction gained, but the lost satisfaction from the forgone alternative. Society will realise that the real cost of using resources in a particular manner is the sacrifice of not being able to use them differently.

The fundamental economic problem is incapable of complete solution, and economists resort to studying how resources are allocated within those societies. Some world powers have their decision making administered by central bodies on a planned basis while the western world seems to be concentrated on a market economy approach. Any economy dominated by market forces will see decentralised decision making resting with millions of individual consumers and producers whose preferences and action will show through the factor and final goods markets.

The combination of consumers, choosing freely to maximise satisfaction, and profit maximising producers, will supply the consuming public with the type and quantity of goods which interest them most. Although the initial impetus may spring from the demand or supply side, the more utopian *laissez-faire* picture is one of 'consumer sovereignty'. The seemingly independent purchasing decisions of the consuming public are conveyed to the producing firms by the existence of a price mechanism, which results in giving signals to the producers as to the relative merits of concentrating on certain products. The self-interest of the producers does the rest as the lure of more profit encourages more goods to be supplied. The very existence of excess demand for a product will result in prices rising, thereby encouraging firms to capitalise on further profit opportunities and bring an expanded supply to the market. Resources once allocated in less profitable fields are now more efficiently utilised, and it has not required a vast administrative complex to bring it about. It was guided as if by 'an invisible hand'. The search for larger and larger profits will create competitive forces encouraging more efficient production from the productive outlets. The gradual lowering of costs will react on prices until a more normal profit situation occurs, and yet the consumers who initiated this process are more than satisfied with their lower priced products.

It is assumed that a perfectly operating market system will result in an efficient and impersonal but optimal allocation of resources. Yet the system outlined falls far short of perfection in the cold, harsh reality of the everyday world, where consumers are often ignorant of opportunities and certainly do not act in the coldly objective, maximum satisfaction seeking manner of the theory. Similarly producers are not always the small competitive units imagined, but are dominating oligopolists within their markets, achieving high profits which do not reflect the degree of competitive efficiency suggested.

Even if these imperfections could be erased, the market system has still a lot to answer for. The unregulated actions of both consumers and producers may well result in the underuse or overuse of the limited resources available resulting in years of instability and depression as seen in the 1930s or even years of inflation and stagnation as seen in the 1970s.

A free market economy might lead to goods of a generally undesirable nature emerging while some of the basic necessities of life remain still born—drugs versus housing and health facilities. There are some goods and services which are not so easily exchanged in the market place—defence and police—and it is questionable whether a market-based system would allow an adequate production of them. Not only should these goods and services be provided collectively, but they are not easily priced and difficulties arise in differentiating between who will benefit from them.

Cases emerge where the prices of goods do not indicate the true benefit or cost to society as a whole, and externalities or spillover effects occur. Market decisions tend to be narrowly commercial neglecting the important external costs and benefits. For example, an increased demand for chemicals while resulting in increased production and profits may involve a wide-scale pollution effect within the atmosphere. The private benefit to the firm as seen in revenue might be high, but would still not exceed the gigantic social cost involved in terms of pollution of the air, buildings and clothes, etc. The pattern of prices within an economy does not reflect the interests of society as a whole and an optimum allocation of resources will certainly not result.

We expect the price system to reflect consumer demands thereby allocating resources efficiently, but consumer demand is based on spending power, and if there is an inequitable distribution of income to begin with, the main force of the spending power will be coming from the people with the most income. It must be left to society to judge for itself the particular merits of the current income structure.

Comments

A. Specific points

1. Division of the essay into **two** sections
   a. What is the basic economic problem?
   How does the market mechanism work?

   b. What are the major difficulties linked to the market economy?

   An equal emphasis should be placed on either section, with candidates producing at least three or four items in the latter half.

2. Points of emphasis

   a. The fundamental problem makes no distinction as to the type of economy considered. Countries of varying political persuasions cannot escape the basic problem of scarcity. Remember, scarcity does not mean a limited supply.

   b. The terms that follow are all interrelated—scarcity; choice; opportunity cost; and allocation of resources. The decision making of all economies is concerned with choice and the preferences shown. The cost of producing anything must be considered in real terms, i.e. the opportunity cost of the resources which have to be foregone. The allocation and reallocation of resources which emerge in societies is the outcome of a series of decisions made partly by the private sector, but these days mostly influenced by the public sector.

   c. The operation of the market mechanism includes an understanding of the following relationships:
      i. independent, unrelated consumer decisions finally result in a magically coordinated effort which will affect demand and supply;
      ii. the self-interest shown by consumers and producers will help to promote the welfare of society as a whole;
      iii. prices help to transmit consumer demand into producer action;
      iv. utility seeking consumers are matched by profit searching producers;
      v. resources are allocated so that consumer preferences are satisfied;
      vi. competitive firms allow costs to be reduced where possible, so that consumers may obtain their purchases at the lowest possible price.

   d. The market economy is by no means perfect. The many flaws include:
      i. cyclical disorders occur resulting in inflationary and deflationary conditions;
      ii. competitive conditions are diminished by monopolistic tendencies both among unions and firms;
      iii. prices may not reflect the social costs and benefits;
      iv. inequalities in the distribution of income set the pattern for the decision making within an economy.

B. General points

1. Check your understanding of the related concepts:

   a. mixed economy   **e.** wants
   b. command economy   **f.** economic goods
   c. production possibility curve   **g.** free goods
   d. utility   **h.** opportunity cost

2. To what extent is 'consumer sovereignty' a thing of the past?
   Inroads into this concept in the twentieth century have come from two areas:
   a. *The rational consumer*, slavishly calculating and objectively demanding goods
   based on a clear scale of preferences, is rarely seen today. We are often ignorant
   of what we are buying and instead are informed by firms of the essential qualities
   of these products by cleverly constructed and revenue gaining advertisement.
   The consumers end up as puppets in the hands of the large companies.
   b. *The small independent firms* still exist today, but they are dwarfed in terms of
   sales, profit and power by the large battalions. Structural changes have meant
   that the oligopolistic form is the characteristic of modern industry, and here
   firms holding dominant market positions tend to fix their own prices rather than
   accept them from the market. Profits do not tend to show how efficiently firms
   are using resources, but merely the degree of their monopoly positions.

3. What is the opportunity cost of reading this book?
   Candidates have a choice between work and play, and within any twenty-four
   hour period, the opportunity cost of working at expanding one's economic
   knowledge is the time given up when one could have been watching the television.
   This can be illustrated by the use of a production possibility curve which indicates
   the alternatives facing the budding economist. (See Fig. 1.) By spending the entire

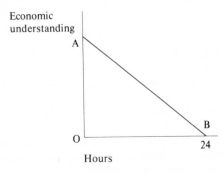

Fig. 1

day at work the pupil will be able to achieve OA's worth of economic knowledge,
but no time for leisure or sleep. On the other hand, the lure of the television and
other leisure pursuits might take priority with no concern for improvement in one's
economic comprehension. Points on the line signify all the combinations of work
and leisure which are possible.

In the example given in Fig. 1, an extra hour's work will always bring the same extra amount of economic understanding. The opportunity cost of giving up one hour's worth of leisure is *constant* in terms of economic understanding achieved. In the real world it is a fact that students are just as likely to succumb to diminishing returns to work as they increase the time spent on their studies. In this case the production possibility curve should be a line drawn convex to the origin, as shown in Fig. 2.

Here, it can be seen that at point G there is a trade off between leisure and economic understanding. But as the movement from G to F continues with equal periods of time given over to work, the degree of *extra* understanding diminishes i.e. LM > MN and MN > NP. In other words, the opportunity cost of an extra amount of economic knowledge in terms of hours of leisure given up, *increases*.

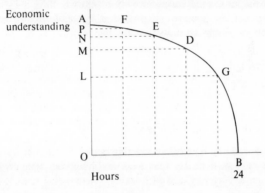

Fig. 2

Essay questions

1. *Show how market forces operate to reach a solution to the economic problem of matching scarce resources to multifarious wants.*   *(O/C Boards)*

2. *Is the consumer 'sovereign' in a modern capitalist economy?*   *(JMB)*

3. *What would you regard as the main strengths and weaknesses of the market system?*   *(ICWA)*

4. *'All economies are confronted with the same fundamental economic problems'. Indicate the nature of these problems and show clearly the different methods used to solve them in market and planned economies.*   *(JMB)*

5. *Explain how the pricing mechanism operates within the economic system. Why does it need to be modified at times by Government intervention?*   *(SU)*

6. *What do you understand by the term 'opportunity cost'? How is it related to the problem of scarcity?*   *(Lond)*

Brief comments on essay questions

Most of the essay questions above can be treated similarly in approach, and contain many points which are common to each other.

a. **What is the basic economic problem?**

  i. *It is a problem of scarcity*—people's wants cannot be satisfied because the resources capable of satisfying these wants are limited, and so the goods produced from these resources are 'scarce'.

  ii. *It is a problem of supplying 'economic goods'*—if a good is in demand and scarce resources have to be sacrificed to produce it, the good will have a related price. The cost of a good should be seen in terms of the real factors of production which are employed in its production.

  iii. *It is a problem of choice*—as an economy obviously cannot satisfy all the wishes of its inhabitants, a choice of how the limited resources will be allocated has to be made.

b. **How does this resource allocation procedure work?**

The answer depends on how the production decisions are made:
  i. command economies believe that decisions should be taken centrally by state officials.

  ii. market economies believe in an interconnected system of markets with people indicating their preferences by the prices they are prepared to pay for the goods of their choice.

c. **How does the market mechanism work—are there weaknesses?**

The specimen essay has attempted to answer these questions quite fully.

d. **What is meant by the term 'opportunity cost'?**

The term is linked closely with the concepts of scarcity, choice and sacrifice. Any economy which uses its resources in one way will incur a sacrifice if it decides to change its allocation of resources—in terms of the goods which have to be foregone. An inclusion of the following points would be considered appropriate:

  i. *Definition*: the opportunity cost of doing something is the cost in terms of foregone alternatives, i.e. the sacrifice which has to be made.

  ii. *Examples*: decisions taken by consumers, firms and governments all involve the concept of opportunity cost. The schoolboy usually makes a conscious choice of work or play. Entrepreneurs may have to decide whether the cost of more production in terms of polluting the atmosphere is worthwhile. Governments must come to terms with increasing their share of the national income at the expense of the private sector in the economy.

iii. *Production Possibility Curves*: opportunity cost can be illustrated graphically by the use of these curves, which indicate the maximum combination of goods an economy or firm is capable of producing when all its resources are efficiently utilised and fully employed.

Suggestions for further reading

Cairncross, A. K. *Introduction to Economics*. (Butterworth, 1973.) Chapters 1–2

Donaldson, P. *Economics of the Real World*. (Penguin, 1973.) Chapters, 2, 11, 12

Giles, C., ed. *Understanding Economics*. (The Manchester Economics Project—Ginn & Co, 1971.) Chapter 1

Harbury, C. D. *An Introduction to Economic Behaviour*. (Fontana/Collins, 1971.) Chapter 3

Harvey, J. *Modern Economics*. (Macmillan, 1974.) Chapters 1–2

Livesey, F. *A Textbook of Economics* (Polytech Publishers Ltd) Chapters 1–2, 22

Stanlake, G. F. *Introductory Economics* (Longman, 1971.) Chapters 1–2

Essay number 2

Comment on the ways in which variables, other than tastes, cause changes in an individual's demand schedule for a commodity.   (O/C Board)

Suggested answer

An individual's demand schedule for a commodity is a statistical table relating the price of the commodity to the demand for it per unit of time. Demand is not merely a desire to purchase something but has to have monetary backing, i.e. an ability and willingness to purchase goods at various prices. The economist sometimes calls this 'effective demand'.

Perhaps the most important factor affecting the demand for a commodity is its price, and most commodities illustrate an inverse relationship between price and quantity demanded. One can then produce a demand schedule in statistical form, which can be reproduced in graph form (see Fig. 1) to give a demand curve usually exhibiting a tendency to slope

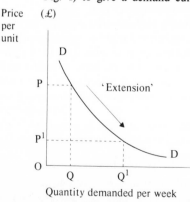

Fig. 1   Fig. 2

downwards to the right. The demand curve in the diagram will then tell us that if the price fell from OP to OP¹, the demand would *extend* from OQ to OQ¹. The demand schedule has not altered or shifted; it is merely a case of more being demanded at a lower price than at a higher price.

There are obviously many other variables likely to affect a commodity's demand, but the demand curve is usually drawn on the assumption that these other factors will remain unchanged and constant. The whole idea of *ceteris paribus* is essential to the validity of such demand curves.

The three most important variables likely to affect an individual's demand schedule for a commodity are incomes, tastes and the prices of related goods, and when these change so will the demand for the good change, shifting the demand curve to the right or left. This increase or decrease in demand is a completely different movement from an extension or contraction of demand. In fact, a different quantity is being demanded at the same price with this whole effect being brought about by a change in one or other of the 'conditions of demand'. Figure 2 illustrates an increase in demand by a movement of the demand curve from D to D¹. This indicates that at price OP, demand has now *increased* from OQ to OQ¹.

A person's income plays a large part in decision making, and the amount of disposable real income gives a far more accurate picture of this determinant. A person's money income can be affected by direct taxation and national insurance contributions along with granted benefits such as family allowances, but the amount remaining, the disposable money income, can still give a false picture unless prices have remained unchanged. It is real income which is important. Any rise in this income can lead to two completely opposite results depending on the good in question, and the income level of the purchaser. Normally, a rise in income, *ceteris paribus*, would result in an increase in demand indicated by a shift of the demand curve to the right. Goods, such as television sets, washing-machines and motor cars, fall into this category, and the final result will probably be a rise in the price of these commodities. However, certain 'inferior' goods, i.e. relatively cheap but inferior substitutes for some other goods, would show a decrease in demand following a rise in income. Some of the basic foodstuffs may illustrate this.

Not only will demand normally increase after a rise in income, but dependent upon the type of good, demand might be very responsive to the change in income. This income elasticity of demand tends to be higher for durable goods such as cars and refrigerators, while services tend to be exceptionally responsive to income changes. Most goods have a positive income elasticity of demand, but inferior goods would show a negative income elasticity of demand.

The demand for a commodity is also affected by a change in the price of closely related goods, the direction of demand depending on whether they are competitive or complementary goods.

Assuming that a person regards tea and coffee as close substitutes, a fall in the price of tea (caused by an increase in supply) will result in a decrease in the demand for coffee. In Fig. 3 the price of tea has fallen from OP to OP¹ and this results in the demand for coffee (Fig. 4) shifting from

DD to D¹D¹. One should be able to measure the cross-elasticity of demand between the two products as a small percentage change in the price of tea might result in a larger percentage change in the demand for coffee, resulting in a positive cross-elasticity of more than unity. It is positive because of the direct relationship between price and demand.

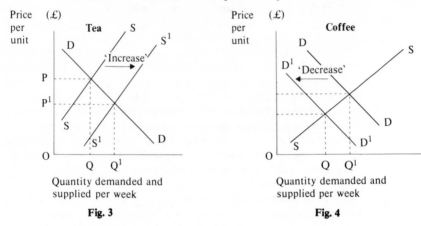

Fig. 3   Fig. 4

However with complementary goods, such as cars and petrol (where the use of one good implies the use of the other), a fall in the price of one good may well result in an increase in the demand for the other—as shown in Figs. 5 and 6. Thus a fall in the price of motor cars may result in an extension in the demand for cars. With people buying more cars, there will obviously be a greater desire to purchase petrol. The increased demand for petrol will be indicated by a shift to the right of the demand curve. This time the cross-elasticity of demand would become a negative figure, because of the inverse relationship between price and demand.

Finally, an individual's demand for a commodity can be affected quite noticeably by his ability to obtain credit, and the changes which occur in

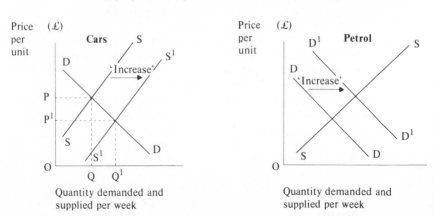

Fig. 5   Fig. 6

hire-purchase regulations can have a significant influence on a person's spending power. This allied to the emotive influence of the advertising world can have startling effects on a person's pattern of spending power.

Comments

A. Specific points

1. Division of the essay into **three** sections

   a. Explain the 'demand schedule'—only a paragraph or two should be necessary.

   b. Explain the relationship between income and demand.

   c. Explain the relationship between prices of related goods and demand.

   The two sections **b.** and **c.** should form the major part of the essay.

2. Points of Emphasis

   a. Clarify the important distinction between:

   i. a change in demand;
   ii. a change in quantity demanded.

   b. The question asks for comment on an individual not a market demand curve. Certain factors which affect market demand can be ignored e.g. an increase in total population, changes in age distribution.

   c. The main variables to concentrate upon are:

   i. income level;

   ii. complementary goods;

   iii. competitive goods.

   The term 'comment' in the title gives candidates an opportunity to develop the income section with some development of the effect of a rise in income on goods regarded as 'inferior'.

   d. Candidates may introduce the concept of elasticity of demand when discussing the main variables, but this must be regarded as a bonus point and efforts must be made to concentrate on *how* the variables affect the demand curve and not by *how much*.

   e. Diagrams should be part of a candidate's armoury in the attempt to clarify complex relationships which are not quite so obvious, when expressed verbally. This particular essay lends itself to the inclusion of a number of simple diagrams.

B. General points

1. Check you understanding of the related concepts:

   a. inverse relationship   **d.** *ceteris paribus*
   b. change in demand   **e.** inferior goods
   c. change in quantity demanded   **f.** cross-elasticity formula.

2. Points of confusion with many candidates:

   a. *Does an extension in demand lead to a rise in price?*

Even though many candidates appreciate the distinction between 'an increase in demand' and 'an extension in demand', they are still confused over their relationships with the price of the good.

The demand for a good *extends* because the price has fallen. The price change has to precede the extension in demand. It is absolutely wrong to believe that an extension in demand leads to a rise in price. The textbooks do not help clear understanding of this area as one sometimes sees such a statement as, 'let us assume that there has been a rise in the price of good X,' without an explanation of the reason for this price rise.

The price rise could have originated from:

  i. a decrease in supply;

  ii. an increase in demand;

  iii. suppliers raising the price above the equilibrium level.

Different reasons for the price rise will lead to different effects on demand and supply conditions.

In **i.** the effect of the price rise would be a contraction of demand.

In **ii.** the effect of the price rise would be an extension of supply.

In **iii.** the effect of the price rise would be a contraction of demand and an extension of supply, but ultimately the price would be forced back to the equilibrium level.

Produce your own diagrams and attempt to work through the effects in each case.

   b. *Does an increase in demand always lead to a rise in price?*

Once an equilibrium price has emerged in a market, it will remain at that level until there is some change in the demand or supply conditions. But an *increase in demand* will not necessarily result in a rise in price unless it is assumed that the supply conditions remain unchanged.

Consider the sequence of events when the conditions of supply remain constant:

  i. an increase in demand—this leads to a shift in the demand curve to the right;

  ii. in the very short run—there is a rise in price as supply is fixed;

  iii. in the short run—suppliers attempt to supply more at the higher price;

  iv. in the short run—a position of excess supply occurs at that price;

  v. in the short run—suppliers are forced to reduce the price until a new position of equilibrium is reached.

Initially an equilibrium price of OP (see Fig. 7) is established. Assume there is an increase in demand following a rise in incomes. In the very short run (when supply is fixed) a position of excess demand emerges of QQ¹ which forces up the price as consumers are prepared to pay much more for the good. In the short run suppliers use their fixed capacity and begin to produce more of the product in the search for higher profits. At a price of OP^1 the suppliers are prepared to produce OQ^1 even though the consumers would demand OQ. A position of excess supply has resulted. The suppliers will be forced to reduce the price until it reaches OP^2 where an equilibrium position has been established.

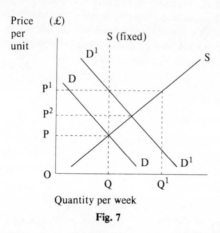

Fig. 7

Consider the sequence of events when simultaneous changes occur in demand and supply. Assume two distinct sets of changes:

i. *An increase in demand and an increase in supply.* A fall in the cost of production and a rise in the public's income will result in the demand and the supply curves shifting to the right. The outcome will *definitely* be an increase in the quantity bought and sold. But the price level *could be* one of three positions—lower, higher or the same level. Everything depends on the extent of the shift in both curves. This is illustrated in the three diagrams on page 30, indicating an industry operating under conditions of increasing returns (or falling costs), decreasing returns (or rising costs) and constant returns (or constant costs).

ii. *An increase in demand and a decrease in supply.* Draw your own diagrams to illustrate the above conditions (Figs 8–10), and show that under these circumstances the price of the commodity will *always* rise but the quantity of the commodity bought and sold might rise, fall or remain the same, dependent on the relative shifts in the demand and supply curves.

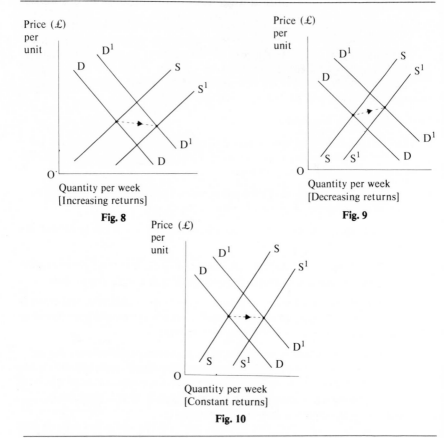

Fig. 8 — [Increasing returns]

Fig. 9 — [Decreasing returns]

Fig. 10 — [Constant returns]

Essay Questions

1. *Explain what an economist means by:*

   a. *'the short period'*
   b. *'the long period'.*

   Using these concepts, analyse the effects of an increase in demand on the price and the supply of a commodity.   (IB)

2. *What factors determine changes in the demand for a product? What problems arise in the real world for a firm seeking to estimate demand?   (Lond.)*

3. *Distinguish between changes in demand and changes in the quantity demanded.   (O/C Board)*

4. *In what ways do market and individual demand curves for a given commodity differ?   (O/C Board)*

5. *Estimate the short-term and long-run effect of a sudden rise of 25% in*

living standards on the price of **a.** *potatoes,* **b.** *imported tomatoes.* *(AEB)*

Brief comments on essay questions

Question 1:

Brief explanation of time periods

a. 'short period'—it is *not* a specific period of time in terms of days, weeks etc, but is the ability to operate within a fixed capacity. Extra production can be obtained only by using more of the variable factors.

b. 'long period'—it is a period of time within which capacity can be changed with sufficient time elapsing so that all factors can be varied.

The demand analysis should occupy the central part of the essay. It can be divided into three sections:

i. *Very Short Period (fixed supply)*—an increase in demand in these circumstances will produce a condition of excess demand resulting in a sharp rise in price.

ii. *Short Period*—the suppliers try to produce more at this higher price and create a position of excess supply at this high price. Gradually the suppliers are forced to lower the price until an equilibrium position emerges.

iii. *Long Period*—if demand is considered to be permanent, suppliers may expand their capacities so that supply can be increased. The supply curve will shift to the right but the final outcome on price will depend on the conditions under which the industry is operating. If economies of scale are being achieved, costs can be reduced with prices falling. However if the industry operates under conditions of decreasing returns (diseconomies of scale), costs will rise and prices will rise also.

Question 3:

This is a relatively straightforward question, but the terminology involved can cause confusion. Although textbooks concentrate on this theme, there does not appear to be a unified approach in the choice of words used. Terms such as 'rise', 'expand', 'extend' and 'increase' have been used in connection with the theme, and many candidates find great difficulty in distinguishing between them.

Both parts to the question should be given equal importance, and it is probably easier to begin with the second of the two terms: 'a change in the quantity demanded'.

a. Change in the quantity demanded

i. Definition of *demand*—demand means 'demand at a price'.

ii. Explanation of a *demand curve*—this is a graphical expression of a demand schedule (which is a table relating price to quantity demanded). But the demand for a commodity can be affected by factors other than price. These factors (or variables) are assumed to be constant (*ceteris paribus*) when demand schedules are being produced.

iii. Explanation of the *direction of a normal demand curve*—the curve illustrates the 'law of demand' in that more is bought at a lower price than at a higher price. This 'extension' in demand (or increase in the quantity demanded) is caused by a fall in price, and the reason for this movement along the demand curve can be more fully developed by expanding on the concept of diminishing marginal utility.

b. Change in demand

i. This involves a complete shift in the demand curve so that more or less is being demanded at the same price.

ii. There must be an initial change in one or other of the variables ('conditions of demand').

iii. These variables (income, tastes, prices of related goods, population changes etc.) require an explanation, but the time constraint will deny their full development.

Candidates would be well advised to supplement their verbal competence by the use of clear diagrams—particularly in this type of essay question.

Suggestions for further reading

Giles, C., ed. *Understanding Economics*. (The Manchester Economics Project—Ginn & Co, 1971.) Chapter 11

Hewitt, G. *Economics of the Market*. (Fontana/Collins, 1971.) Chapter 2

Harvey, J. *Modern Economics*. (Macmillan, 1974.) Chapter 3

Lipsey, R. G. *An Introduction to Positive Economics*. (Weidenfeld & Nicolson, 1975.) Chapter 7

Livesey, F. *A Textbook of Economics* (Polytech Publishers Ltd, 1978.) Chapter 23

Stanlake, G. F. *Introductory Economics* (Longman, 1971.) Chapter 14

Whitehead, G. *Economics made Simple* (W. H. Allen, 1974.) Chapter 7

Essay number 3

Explain the concept of elasticity of demand, and consider its practical significance. Illustrate your answer by diagrams. (ICWA).

Suggested answer

The concept of elasticity of demand is concerned with the extent of the change in demand, and not the direction of the movement.

In general terms then, the elasticity of demand for a commodity is the responsiveness of the quantity demanded to a small change in the price of that commodity, but it is more accurately defined as the relationship between the proportionate change in the quantity demanded to the proportionate change in price. While absolute changes might give the impression of a high degree of responsiveness, it is in fact the percentage change that matters.

To facilitate measurement the following formula can be given:

$$\text{elasticity of demand} = \frac{\text{percentage change in quantity demanded}}{\text{percentage change in price}}.$$

From this we can accord elasticity of demand a numerical value in that when this ratio is greater than one, demand is elastic, and when the ratio is less than one, demand is inelastic. If the ratios are equal demand has unit elasticity.

It is commonplace to attempt to illustrate this concept by showing a downward sloping straight line demand curve, and stating that a steeply angled one would represent inelastic demand, while a flatter slope would illustrate elastic demand. However, it is vitally important to make clear that demand in fact varies in its elasticity at different points on the demand curve. This can be shown (see Fig. 1) by measuring the percentage change in price and demand at various points, so that it will become obvious that

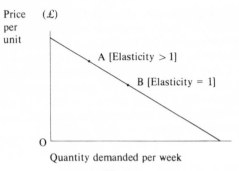

Fig. 1

elasticity of demand at point A is greater than the elasticity of demand at point B.

There are exceptions to this rule and the three diagrams below (Figs 2–4) will illustrate cases where the elasticity of demand is constant at all prices.

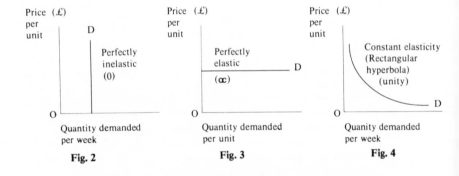

Fig. 2   Fig. 3   Fig. 4

The explanation thus far has concentrated upon the concept of *price* elasticity of demand, but demand also responds to changes in income, and to changes in the price of a related good, i.e. competitive demand or complementary demand. Income elasticity can be explained by looking at the relationship between a percentage change in income and the associated percentage change in demand. For most goods the relationship is a positive one with some being highly income elastic—motor cars, television sets, washing-machines, etc. Some inferior goods show a negative income elasticity.

Where there are two goods closely related, the concept of cross-elasticity can show how the demand for one good can be affected by a price change in the other. Goods which are in competitive demand, such as coffee and tea, rival detergent powders, margarine and butter, etc., will usually have a very high cross-elasticity.

The practical significance of elasticity of demand is related to revenue changes associated with price changes. Elasticity of demand forms part of a businessman's armoury of important commercial data which will ultimately help him in the competitive struggle in which he is engaged. If a supplier correctly assessed that the good he is producing is one of inelastic demand, then by raising its price there is bound to be an increase in his profits. Figure 5 illustrates a demand curve which is relatively inelastic in the price range chosen. When the price is raised from OP to OP¹ (say 10%) demand falls from OQ to OQ¹ (say 2%). This results in an increase in total revenue, and as less would be produced the total costs would fall; hence profits will expand.

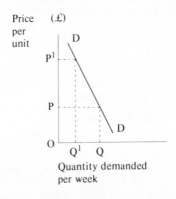

Fig. 5

Nationalised industries must also consider this concept in that any raising of fares on British Rail may have an adverse effect on the operating deficit it is trying to reduce. Rail transport has a rival in the private transport of the motorist and the existence of a substitute will tend to convince rail users that any price increase in rail travel would be met by a complete change of allegiance to the motor car.

The Chancellor of the Exchequer makes use of the differing responses of demand to price changes by adjusting the weapon of indirect taxation. Goods of inelastic demand, such as cigarettes, beer and petrol seem destined to be the ideal agents for use by the Chancellor. If the objective is to raise valuable revenue to finance government expenditure then these goods will bear an increased tax. The unfortunate consumers of these products almost tend to ignore the rise in their prices, so that although demand does diminish slightly, the government still manages to reap the harvest of increased revenue.

Countries on fixed exchange rates must also be aware of the relative elasticities of demand for both their exports and imports, as any attempt to reduce the balance of payments deficit by devaluation might rebound on the advocates of such a policy. Although there are other considerations, the likely success of a devaluation depends on the relative elasticities of demand and supply of both exports and imports. Devaluation will make a country's exports cheaper in world markets and its imports dearer. As each unit of exports is now cheaper in terms of foreign

currency, demand must be relatively elastic for the total of foreign currency earned to rise. With imports being dearer in terms of sterling, the UK
would look for its imports to have an elastic demand, as in that case the
amount of foreign currency spent on imports will be reduced. Although
the depreciation of sterling in recent years has given our exporters a competitive edge, the major problem seems to be the relatively inelastic demand for imports thereby helping to fuel the cost inflation already present
in the economy.

Comments

A. Specific points

1. Division of the essay into two sections:

   a. Explanation of the concept of elasticity of demand, including income and cross-
   elasticity but giving the major portion of this section over to price elasticity.

   b. The practical significance of the concept to various groups of people or institutions—consumers, producers and government.

   Candidates will have alternatives as to the significance of either section, but one
   would be advised to give roughly equal treatment to the sections.

2. Points of Emphasis:

   a. A distinction must be made between *absolute* and *percentage* changes in order to
   show that the slope of the curve is not that important, and can positively mislead
   candidates in their true understanding of this concept.

   b. The three demand elasticities must be mentioned, but justice can only be done to
   one of them—price elasticity—in this type of essay.

   c. Price elasticity is elasticity at a price, indicating that the elasticity of demand
   differs at different points on a demand curve—there are exceptions!

   d. The practical applications of the concept are firmly linked with total revenue
   changes.

B. General points

1. Check your understanding of the related terms:

   a. unit elasticity   d. negative cross-elasticity
   b. arc elasticity   e. point elasticity
   c. income elasticity   f. rectangular hyperbola.

2. Some common points of confusion:

   a. *Which method of elasticity is correct?*
   The proportionate changes in price and demand can be utilised in two ways:

      i. to give a numerical value of elasticity;

      ii. to give a relationship between elasticity and revenue.

However, a comparison of these methods appears to give different results on occasions. For example, when elasticity of demand is unity the change in total revenue should be nil after a price change. If a good falls in price from £5 to £4 (a 20% change), and the quantity demanded increases from 10 units to 12 units (a 20% change), the total revenue in fact will fall from £50 to £48. This does not seem in accord with the idea that lowering the price of a good of inelastic demand will result in a reduction in total revenue. In the above case of unit elasticity there should have been an unchanged total revenue.

This apparent inconsistency can be answered by realising that elasticity of demand is only valid when there is a small percentage change in price. One can see that total revenue will be practically unchanged the smaller the percentage change in price and quantity becomes. Make up an example involving a 1% change in price and quantity and see how little the total revenue changes.

b. *How should you calculate a percentage change?*
It is customary to begin by finding the percentage change in price and dividing it into the percentage change in demand. When one calculates the percentage price change it is normal practice to show the price change as a percentage of the original price. In this case one will obtain a different numerical elasticity figure dependent on the direction of movement of the price change. For instance, a fall in price from £10 to £9 is a 10% change, but a rise in price from £9 to £10 is a 11.1% change. A way round the problem can be obtained by allowing the change in price (£1) to be divided by the average price (£9.50). This will enable a percentage change of 10.5% to be obtained, and for the elasticity between two points on the same curve to be a single value irrespective of the direction of movement between the two points.

c. *How important is the sign?*
By using the accepted formula for price elasticity we can obtain a numerical value of elasticity for a particular good. The more responsive demand is to a price change, the more elastic is the good said to be. One would want therefore to equate 'more responsive' with a larger value. However as demand curves usually slope downwards to the right, a price change will always have the opposite sign to the demand change. Under normal circumstances then, a good which is responsive in demand would have a high number but preceded by a minus sign. This causes some confusion when comparing the elasticities of two goods, the more responsive of which has the larger number but is also preceded by a negative sign. Is -10 a smaller value than -5? By convention a minus sign is placed in front of the formula (look carefully for it in your text book) so that the final value is made into a positive number.

3. The importance of income elasticity of demand:

Statisticians have found that estimates of the income elasticity of demand for various foodstuffs tend to be less than unity but mostly positive e.g. butter $=0.46$. This would illustrate a traditional tendency for the demand for food to rise less rapidly than income, which is an important consideration for food exporting countries. In forecasting future sales at any given price, producers will have to include in their assessments the predicted change in the general level of incomes. Producers of products with an income elasticity of demand of less than unity cannot expect to keep up with the growth rate in the economy as a whole unless they reduce prices sufficiently so as to compensate for the slow rise in demand.

Essay questions

1. *Define the terms 'price elasticity', 'income elasticity' and 'cross-elasticity of demand'. What would you be able to infer about the demand for a commodity when given the magnitudes (and signs where relevant) of these elasticities? (O/C Board)*

2. **a.** *Discuss briefly what is measured by the concept of price elasticity of demand and indicate its uses in certain areas of economic analysis.*

   b. *Explain why (using the example of a straight line downward sloping demand curve) it may be inaccurate to refer to the price elasticity of a 'demand curve'. (WJEC)*

3. *Why would you expect the price and income elasticities of demand for petroleum to be higher in some markets than in others? Analyse the effects of a substantial increase in the import price of petroleum on the main British users. (Camb.)*

4. *Explain whether and why you would expect the demand for foreign holidays to be relatively elastic or inelastic to changes in their price. How is a fall in the foreign exchange rate likely to affect the demand for foreign holidays? (JMB)*

Brief comments on essay questions

Question 4

The question should be divided into two parts (two thirds of the time being devoted to the first section). The following format might be applicable.

1. **Introduction:** A definition of elasticity of demand making it clear that percentage changes and not absolute changes, are called for.

   —A diagram containing a linear downward sloping demand curve illustrating that price elasticity of demand varies at various prices.

2. **Application:** An indication how some determinants of the elasticity of demand can be related to the demand for foreign holidays.

   i. Availability of close substitutes: this could be the comparison of a holiday in the UK or even the purchase of a colour television/deep freezer etc. The greater the degree of substitution the more elastic demand for foreign holidays will be. There are people who would not consider a British holiday as an alternative—in this case demand for foreign holidays is inelastic. The lure of sun soaked beaches in Europe cannot be substituted!

ii. The luxury status of a foreign holiday—travelling abroad must certainly be considered expensive and a luxury by the average holiday maker, and that being so, the demand for such holidays is extremely responsive to price.

iii. The greater the proportion of a person's income which is spent on foreign holidays—a poorer person who puts aside a considerable percentage of income to enjoy the delights of foreign shores will react differently to a richer person who may not have had the concern of saving a large proportion of his income. A richer person may regard the holiday as a necessity!

iv. If the excitement and satisfaction obtained from a foreign holiday is habit forming, people may make a more conscious effort to save sufficient funds and ignore any price increases in the package deal.

3. The exchange rate: people require foreign currency to go abroad, and it has to be purchased by the exchange of sterling. Any fall in the exchange rate will make it more expensive to acquire the foreign currency necessary to make the journey. This is likely to cut the demand for such foreign holidays. Although the domestic price level in the foreign country has not changed, the fall in the exchange rate has meant that a tourist is paying more to transport himself overseas. A holiday initially costing \$300 in foreign currency will be more expensive if the rate of exchange falls from £1 = \$3 to £1 = \$1.5. Our tourist would have to find £200 to acquire the necessary dollars.

Suggestions for further reading

Cairncross, A. K. *Introduction to Economics.* (Butterworth, 1973.) Chapter 14

Giles, C., ed. *Understanding Economics.* (The Manchester Economics Project—Ginn & Co., 1971.) Chapter 11

Harbury, C. D. *An Introduction to Economic Behaviour.* (Fontana/Collins, 1971.) Chapter 4

Harvey, J. *Modern Economics.* (Macmillan, 1974.) Chapter 5

Lipsey, R. G. *An Introduction to Positive Economics.* (Weidenfeld & Nicolson, 1975.) Chapter 10

Livesey, F. *A Textbook of Economics.* (Polytech Publishers Ltd, 1978.) Chapter 23

Stanlake, G. F. *Introductory Economics.* (Longman, 1971.) Chapter 14

Whitehead, G. *Economics Made Simple.* (W. H. Allen, 1974.) Chapter 10

Essay number 4

Explain what is meant in the analysis of consumer behaviour by the term 'an inferior good'. Consider how a consumer might react to a fall in the price of a good he considers to be inferior. (WJEC)

Suggested answer

The demand for a good can be affected by a great number of different variables including price, income, tastes and the prices of related goods. With most goods, a rise in income, other things being equal, will normally be followed by a rise in the demand for those goods. This can be thought of as a positive income effect.

A rise in real income can emerge in two ways. The money income of a consumer might increase, other things remaining unchanged, or a fall in the price of a good could occur, money incomes remaining constant. In both respects the consumer's real income has increased i.e. his ability to purchase goods and services has risen, and for most goods this increased buying power will be used to buy more items.

There are some goods however, usually low quality goods, which will fall in demand as real income increases. In fact, we can say that demand varies inversely with income giving a negative income effect. Consumers tend to replace these goods with more high quality goods as their income rises. Goods such as margarine and potatoes are often replaced by other foodstuffs, while motor cycles are often replaced by motor cars as income rises. Figure 1 illustrates the demand for an inferior good, where at incomes below ON the demand may be rising, but after point ON has been reached the demand decreases, the good possibly being replaced by a more expensive substitute which can now be afforded.

When a good falls in price, two major influences are set in motion: a substitution effect and an income effect. The substitution effect is quite simply a change in the relative price of the good, and a fall in price will mean that because it is now relatively cheaper, a consumer will switch his

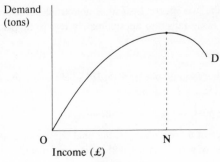

Fig. 1

spending power from the expensive to the cheaper good. This change in price will also affect the consumer's real income as he is now better off and capable of purchasing a larger volume of the good.

Normally these two forces work in the same direction encouraging the consumer to buy more of a good when the price falls. But if the consumer considers the good to be inferior the two effects may clash and begin to work in an opposing manner. While the substitution effect would still indicate that a consumer would switch his spending power to the relatively cheaper priced good, the real income effect in this case would become negative.

The overall effect on the demand for the good after a price fall will depend on the relative strengths of the two opposing forces. If the consumer spends a small fraction of his income on the good, there is not likely to be much of an income effect anyway, and so the income effect will be outweighed by the substitution effect, resulting in a rise in demand. But if the consumer spends a large proportion of his income on the good, the income effect which is negative is likely to overwhelm the substitution effect, and result in a fall in demand. A commodity which exhibits this tendency is called a 'Giffen good', taken from the work of Sir Robert Giffen whose researches indicated that certain goods were demanded more when they were dear than when they were cheap. Goods of low quality, forming an important element in the expenditure of the poor, could at times exhibit this tendency.

Comments
A. Specific points
1. Division of the essay into **two** sections:

   a. Define an 'inferior good'—usually related to changes in income.

   b. A price fall can result in two effects occurring:

      i. substitution

      ii. income.

In this essay it was decided not to use indifference curve analysis to explain the

difference between the two effects. Instead, a non-graphical approach has been
adopted, where the essay falls into approximately two equal parts.

2. Points of Emphasis:

   a. The income effect should not be regarded solely as a money income effect. Price
   changes can affect the real income.

   b. Inferior goods possess negative income effects.

   c. When the price of a good changes, the final change in demand will be the combined outcome of a substitution and an income effect.

   d. A Giffen good is an extreme example of an inferior good. Candidates often fail to
   see the distinction between the two goods, which can be called an 'ordinary inferior good' and a 'Giffen good'.

   e. Inferior goods will still exhibit the tendency of a downward sloping demand
   curve (to the right) but a Giffen good would be illustrated by an exceptional demand curve (a perverse curve).

B. General points

1. Make sure you understand the following terms:

   a. negative income effect   **d.** Giffen goods
   b. real income   **e.** an exceptional demand curve
   c. relative prices   **f.** substitution effect

2. What is meant by an income effect?

   There can be an income effect even if there is no change in money income. As long
   as the price of the good changes, there will be a change in real income (other things
   being equal). So a change in a person's income can occur in two ways:

   a. his money income changes, other things being equal; or

   b. the price level changes, money incomes remaining constant.

   Both **a.** and **b.** will result in a change in real income.
   A rise in real income will result in:

   a. a rise in demand for normal goods;

   b. a fall in demand for inferior goods.

   We can say that normal goods have a positive income effect, while inferior goods
   have a negative income effect.

3. What is meant by the price effect?

   A price change is associated with two side effects:

   a. a substitution effect

   b. real income effect.

It is the combination of these two effects which will determine the eventual slope of the demand curve.

With normal goods (Fig. 2), the effects work in the same direction and complement each other.

With *inferior* goods (Fig. 3), the effects work in opposite directions—in this case the final direction of demand depends on how powerful one effect is compared with the other, and this itself depends on *how great a proportion of income is spent on the good.*

If an inferior good (Fig. 4) shows tendencies for its income effect to outweigh its substitution effect, its demand will fall when the price falls—and vice versa. Such a good is called a 'Giffen good' and has a demand curve which slopes upwards to the right.

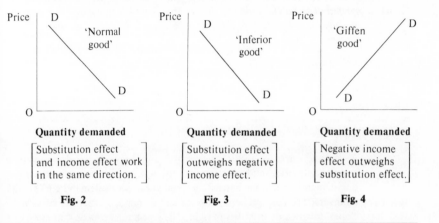

Substitution effect and income effect work in the same direction.	Substitution effect outweighs negative income effect.	Negative income effect outweighs substitution effect.
Fig. 2	**Fig. 3**	**Fig. 4**

Suggestions for further reading

Harvey, J. *Modern Economics*. (Macmillan, 1971.) Chapter 5

Hewitt, G., *Economics of the Market*. (Fontana/Collins, 1976.) Chapter 4

Lipsey, R. G. *An Introduction to Positive Economics*. (Weidenfield & Nicolson, 1975.) Chapter 15, appendix

Livesey, F. *A Textbook of Economics*. (Polytech Publishers Ltd, 1978.) Chapter 23

Powicke, J. C. *Economic Theory*. (Arnold, 1968.) Chapter 6

Whitehead, G. *Economics Made Simple*. (W. H. Allen, 1974.) Chapter 13

Essay number 5

Explain carefully the theoretical analysis underlying the drawing of a normal demand curve sloping downwards from left to right. Are there any reasons for believing that there may be exceptions to this normal diagram?   *(Oxf.)*

Suggested answer

A demand curve is a functional relationship between the demand for a good and its price, and is drawn with the proviso that other factors affecting demand remain unchanged. Normal goods show demand curves with an inverse relationship between price and demand, so that the curve itself slopes downwards from left to right. The graph then tells us that more of a good will be bought at a lower price than at a higher one.

Why do people buy goods anyway? Consumers are striving for satisfaction from the goods they purchase, and if we assume rationality among consumers they will be purchased until maximum satisfaction is achieved. We use the word 'utility' to signify satisfaction. Utility is the ability of a good to give satisfaction to a consumer.

As a consumer obtains more of a good his total utility will rise, but it has been found that each successive unit of the good will give him less and less extra satisfaction. His total utility will rise but at a diminishing rate. A person coming out of the desert would obtain tremendous utility from the first glass of water available, but the second and third glass of water would inevitably give less satisfaction than the first glass.

We can illustrate this concept in diagrammatic form. Figure 1 indicates a total utility curve, assuming we can measure the immeasurable. This will rise as more is consumed but at a decreasing rate until further consumption might lead to total utility actually diminishing. Figure 2 purports to indicate the amount of utility gained from purchasing successive units of a commodity. Marginal utility is the satisfaction a consumer receives from acquiring an extra unit, and it is shown that a consumer obtains less extra satisfaction from successive units of the good until a point is reached

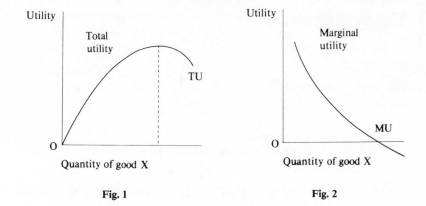

Fig. 1   Fig. 2

where further units actually give negative marginal utility, sometimes called disutility.

In maximising his satisfaction from his purchase a consumer will attempt to maximise his total utility or in other words, to try to obtain units until the marginal utility becomes zero. While this might be true concerning free goods i.e. goods for which no price need be paid, most goods have to be paid for and one is faced with the problem of how to distribute one's expenditure so as to maximise one's total utility. The consumer must allocate his expenditure between the various goods at his disposal in such a way that finally he would not want to switch a single penny of his outlay from one good to another. This means that the last penny he spends on good A will bring him the same marginal utility as the last penny he spends on good B.

To achieve this equilibrium position the consumer would have to vary the quantity bought of each good, realising that the more he buys of one good, the marginal utility of that good will fall. The reallocation of expenditure would mean that a reduction on the other good would cause its marginal utility to rise. This adjustment would continue until the marginal utility obtained from each good purchased would be in the same relationship to price, a concept known as the law of equi-marginal returns:

i.e. $$\frac{\text{MU of a unit of X}}{\text{price of a unit of X}} = \frac{\text{MU of a unit of Y}}{\text{price of a unit of Y}}.$$

Assuming the consumer is in the equilibrium position, as noted above, and the price of good X falls, other things being equal, the consumer is in the happy position of being able to obtain more units of X for that last penny spent on it, i.e. his marginal utility for the last penny spent on X is now greater than the marginal utility for the last penny spent on good Y. His equilibrium position has been altered, and he has to readjust his expenditure pattern so as to regain equilibrium and thus to maximise his total utility. He must seek to realign the utility he gets from the last penny spent on both goods by buying more of X which will reduce his marginal utility for X and reducing his spending on Y which will increase his marginal utility for Y.

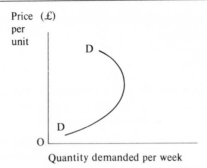

Fig. 3

There are cases of course where demand curves slope in the opposite direction indicating that more is demanded the higher the price. Figure 3 illustrates this perverse demand curve which may only operate over a limited price range, and can be seen in the demand for ostentatious goods, such as diamonds, fur coats, etc. These goods may be bought as status symbols and a fall in their price might result in a reduction in their appeal with the demand going down. Whether the total demand finally goes down will depend upon the extent of the fall in price, and the widening of the market to a lower income group.

Another example of this exceptional demand curve could be people's reactions to changes in security prices. The price of securities on the Stock Exchange is determined fundamentally by the interaction of decisions from buyers and sellers, and excessive demand for shares will inevitably result in their prices rising. This rise in price may well lead to speculators anticipating further price rises and they might buy even more shares before the explosion occurs. Falling share prices do not attract the normal investor as he is convinced the fall will continue.

Finally, the existence of inferior goods provides another example why the demand for a good and its price may be in direct relationship with each other. There are some goods such as the basic foodstuffs of underdeveloped countries, where consumption may fall as income rises. When the price of these goods falls, the real income effect is such as to effect an increase in income, and as people feel themselves better off they may prefer to divert some of their expenditure from the staple foodstuffs towards more expensive and attractive foods. Goods, such as potatoes, rice, bread, etc., when comprising the greater percentage of families' incomes, may exhibit this tendency of an exceptional demand curve, and are often called Giffen goods.

Comments

A. Specific points

1. Division of the essay into **two** sections:

   a. The concept of marginal utility which lies behind the shape of the demand curve—this should take the main portion of this essay.

b. Reasons for perverse demand curves—probably a paragraph on each of the three main reasons.

2. Points of Emphasis:

   a. The underlying theme in the first part of this essay is the reason why the demand curve slopes downwards to the right—or why is the demand for a commodity higher at a lower price than at a higher one?

   b. The concept of the margin and the law of diminishing marginal utility must be fully explored—the distinction between total and marginal utility confirms the view that economic decision making is at the margin.

   c. Explain the equilibrium position of a consumer showing the relationship between marginal utility of a good and the price of that good. This section demands an accuracy and a clarity that are most difficult to achieve in this area.

   d. A price change will alter the equilibrium position of a consumer, involving a decision on his part to regain a new equilibrium position.

   e. The three main examples of an exceptional demand curve are inferior goods (Giffen goods), goods of ostentation and expected price changes in the future.

B. General points

1. Make sure you understand the following terms:

   a. marginal utility   **d.** law of equi-marginal returns
   b. total utility   **e.** perverse demand curves
   c. diminishing marginal utility   **f.** equilibrium.

2. Some common points of confusion:

   a. *Do we make marginal decisions?*
   Economics has been called the study of choice, with decisions being constantly made. Rational consumers are anxiously trying to increase their total utility of a commodity—in fact it measures the strength of their demand for the *whole supply* of the commodity. But economic choices are seldom of this all or nothing type; normally consumers are faced with the choice of a little more of one good and a little less of another. This marginal concept is fundamental in consumer behaviour and much depends on how much of the product the consumer already possesses. The more we possess a good, the less importance we attach to a further addition to our consumption.

   b. *Can we measure utility?*
   It must surely be impossible to measure the total satisfaction one receives from the consumption of a good or service; you cannot measure 'pleasure'. Even so, some economists have been known to get around this problem by using the term 'util', i.e. a unit of measurement of safisfaction. The same problem is not quite so obvious with the marginal utility of a good, as the satisfaction a consumer receives from the last unit he is prepared to purchase is linked closely with the

price he is prepared to pay for that last unit. For instance, if a consumer is eating cream buns, the more buns consumed, the less is the value he puts on an extra bun. As each bun is priced the same, the consumer will continue to purchase buns until he receives a marginal utility of buns which is identical to the price. He will not go further than this point as he would be purchasing a unit, the satisfaction of which is less than the price he is paying to acquire it. Thus the amount a person pays for the last unit of a good which he consumes, can be taken as a measure of the satisfaction which that marginal unit brings to him.

c. *Does the consumer get a bargain?*

A consumer is usually willing to pay more for something than he is, in fact, asked to do. Producers are however powerless to prevent this consumer from obtaining the goods at the current price, as it is almost impossible to negotiate separately with every consumer for every individual unit sold. While identical units of a product are priced the same, it is well known that consumers may be prepared to pay far more for the first unit rather than go without it altogether. They would act similarly in their assessment of the second unit and so on until they reached a point where the last unit purchased was just worth the price that was being asked.

The difference between what consumers do pay and the amount which they would be willing to pay is called a consumer's surplus. Figure 4 shows an individual demand curve based on a person's demand schedule for cream buns.

Price (p)	Demand
25	0
20	1
15	2
10	3
5	4

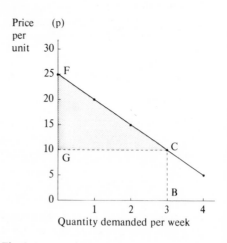

Fig. 4

Assuming the current price of cream buns to be 10p, the consumer would buy three buns and his total outlay would be 30p. However, if each bun were to be separately priced, the consumer would have been prepared to spend 20 + 15 + 10 = 45p to obtain the three buns. The difference (15p) is his consumer's surplus. Total expenditure is indicated by the area OBCG, while total utility obtained from the purchase (expressed in money) is indicated by the area OBCF. The shaded triangular area remaining GCF, is regarded as consumer's suplus. It seems likely that the lower the current price, the larger the consumer's surplus.

d. *Why are diamonds more valuable than water?*

Schoolboy economists and even early economists have often been confused by the fact that an essential commodity such as water has a lower price than a luxury commodity such as diamonds. Surely goods which give a great deal of satisfaction and high total utilities should be expensive, while those with low total utilities should be cheap. The value of a good in the market, its exchange value, must surely be related to how much satisfaction it can give. However, observations in real life showed that this analysis was not the case. Early economists could not find the answer, but this was due to their lack of awareness of the distinction between total utility and marginal utility.

Something as important and life sustaining as water, must obviously have a high total utility. We would give up anything rather than go without water at all. But with water being relatively plentiful, an extra unit of water does not give a great deal of extra utility—in fact, the marginal utility of water is quite low. However the total utility of something like diamonds is very low—it is certainly small in comparison with water. There would be no great hardship if all the diamonds in the world disappeared. But as they are a relatively scarce commodity an additional diamond is well worth having, giving diamonds a high marginal utility.

It is therefore the marginal utility of a commodity and not its total utility which determines its value to a consumer. The greater the quantity of a commodity possessed by a consumer, the lower will be the marginal utility of the good to him, and the less will he be prepared to pay to purchase an extra unit of the good. The law of diminishing marginal utility has a fundamental place in the understanding of price determination.

3. An example:

Although students may appreciate the verbal reasoning which lies behind the law of equi-marginal returns, they become confused when this is translated into mathematical terms. The following questions and answers are given in an attempt to clarify matters.

A rational consumer spends his entire income on two goods, X and Y, reaching the position given below. Which of the following actions will the consumer take?

a. Continue with his present consumption pattern.

b. Buy more X and less Y.

c. Buy more X and the same amount of Y.

d. Buy less X and more Y.

	Good X	Good Y
marginal utility	10	10
price per unit	2p	1p

An equilibrium position is one where the marginal utilities of the two goods are in the same proportion to their prices.

a. Although the marginal utilities of both goods are the same, the prices of the goods are different, and the consumer is certainly not in an equilibrium state. He would not be acting rationally if he took no action to change his spending pattern.

b. Additional units of X would diminish the marginal utility of X; fewer units of Y would increase the marginal utility of Y. We want the ratio of marginal utility to price for both goods to be equal, and this action would take the present ratio of 5:1 for X and 10:1 for Y much further apart.

c. This action is impossible to achieve as the money to purchase more X would have to come from giving up possible expenditure on Y. In any case, even if the consumer dipped into his savings, the additional units of X with the same amount of Y would still help to widen the gap between the two ratios.

d. The consumer would buy less X and more Y, as under these circumstances the marginal utility of X would rise and that of Y would fall until the point was reached where the ratios were equated.

4. Some common misconceptions:

a. The law of diminishing marginal utility is synonomous with the law of diminishing marginal returns.

b. Marginal utility begins to diminish when the total utility obtained from a good starts to fall.

c. A consumer will have reached his equilibrium position when he has distributed his income in such a way as to equate the marginal utility of all goods purchased.

d. All inferior goods (goods with a negative income effect) are known as Giffen goods.

Look *carefully* at these sentences. They are all *false* statements.

a. Utility means satisfaction while returns involves a physical quantity of a commodity. The latter term is connected with the addition of variable factors of production being associated with a fixed factor, such as a factory. By underusing or overusing the capacity, the returns to the variable factor will rise or fall.

b. In most cases, marginal utility will begin to decline as extra units of particular commodities are purchased. A purchaser may still be increasing his total utility under these circumstances but the marginal utility will be positive. If total utility begins to decline then the marginal utility has become negative.

c. The criterion for equilibrium is *not* the equating of marginal utilities of the various goods (unless the goods are all equally priced). If prices differ, then marginal utilities must be in the same proportion to their prices.

d. The main distinction between inferior and Giffen goods is that in the latter the negative income effect outweights the substitution effect so that the demand curve is upward sloping to the right.

Essay questions

1. *A consumer has 20p to spend on two commodities A and B. The table shows the total utility (measured in utils) which he would derive from the two commodities.*

Units of A or B purchased	Total utility of A (in utils)	Total utility of B (in utils)
1	9	10
2	15	18
3	20	24
4	24	28
5	27	29

   a. *Calculate the marginal utility of each unit of A and B.*

   b. *By what principle should the consumer allocate his spending between A and B to maximise utility?*

   c. *How much of the two goods will he buy if their units prices are as follows?*

	Price of A	Price of B
i.	4p	4p
ii.	5p	1p
iii.	3p	1p

   d. *Explain the changing pattern of the consumer's purchases as prices alter by reference to the income and substitution effects. (IB)*

2. *What part does the principle of diminishing marginal utility play in the theory of value? (O/C Board)*

3. *Explain and discuss the statement that the price actually paid for a commodity is a money measure of the marginal utility of that commodity. (IB)*

Brief comments on essay questions

Question 1

This style of question must be answered as concisely as possible. An accurate calculation or explanation is worth more than a longer rambling account.

a. The marginal utility for particular units of A and B can be calculated by seeing how much extra utility can be achieved by purchasing another unit of both goods. This would result in the marginal utilities of A and B respectively being:

9 and 10 for the 1st unit
6 and 8 for the 2nd unit
5 and 6 for the 3rd unit
4 and 4 for the 4th unit
3 and 1 for the 5th unit.

b. A consumer will reach a position of equilibrium in his spending allocation when he has maximised his utility. The law of equi-marginal returns must be adhered to in that the marginal utilities of both goods must be made proportional to their prices. The equation can illustrate this:

$$\frac{\text{MU of A}}{\text{price of A}} = \frac{\text{MU of B}}{\text{price of B}}.$$

c. The utilisation of the equi-marginal returns formula will enable candidates to arrive at the correct answers. Using each pair of prices at each stage, and making sure that they are being compared with marginal utilities (not total utilities), the following answers will emerge:

i. 2A and 3B
ii. 3A and 5B
iii. 5A and 5B.

d. When the pattern of prices alters from **i.** to **ii.,** one can see that B has become relatively cheaper by its price falling and A's price rising. Basing one's findings on the answers to section **c.,** the consumer increased his purchases of B thereby illustrating the substitution principle which is transferring expenditure to items which are relatively cheaper. At the same time the price of A has risen and yet the consumer still manages to purchase more than previously. This illustrates the concept of the income effect in that real income has fallen as far as this good is concerned, and yet more of the good is purchased—a negative income effect.

When prices alter from **ii.** to **iii.** only the substitution effect is at work as more of A is bought when it becomes relatively cheaper.

It is important to remember that when a price change occurs, both substitution and income effects are operating. It is only when a price fall (or rise) is met by less (or more) being demanded that the income effect is seen to be out-weighing the substitution effect.

Suggestions for further reading

Cairncross, A. K. *Introduction to Economics.* (Butterworth, 1973.) Chapter 15

Giles, C., ed. *Understanding Economics.* (The Manchester Economics Project–Ginn & Co., 1971.) Chapter 8

Harvey, J. *Modern Economics.* (Macmillan, 1974.) Chapter 5

Lipsey, R. G., *An Introduction to Positive Economics.* (Weidenfeld & Nicolson, 1975.) Chapter 15

Livesey, F. *A Textbook of Economics.* (Polytech Publishers Ltd., 1970.) Chapter 23

Whitehead, G. *Economics Made Simple.* (W. H. Allen, 1974.) Chapter 7

Essay number 6

'Artificial shortages of goods will always be the result of price controls'.
Discuss. (Oxf.)

The market economy relies on the price mechanism to enable the scarce resources to be allocated efficiently among the many competing uses. The forces of demand and supply help to determine a market price, and if this price were such that the amount the consumers were prepared to buy was greater than the amount suppliers were prepared to offer for sale, a position of excess demand would arise.

Figure 1 illustrates this position as seen at price OP^1 where OM is demanded yet OM^1 is supplied. In a free economy this imbalance would not persist for long as the price would be forced up until it reached OP. This is the equilibrium price. It can be seen that any shortage of a good

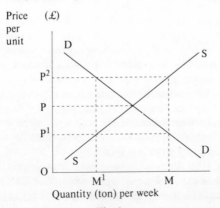

Fig. 1

will disappear because the changes in price will help to ration out this scarce supply.

A government may attempt to intervene in the market economy by legislating on price levels. Laws may be passed to fix a maximum price above which certain goods may not be sold. It may be that the government considered the existing price level to be too high and therefore detrimental to the poorer section of the community. If the government decided on a maximum price of OP^1 to be fixed below the equilibrium price of OP, a situation of excess demand would arise in that OM is greater than OM^1. This legal ceiling of OP^1 has created an artificial shortage of the good to the extent of $M^1 M$. Suppliers may charge less than price OP^1, but this would not solve the problem of the shortage. In fact, at the controlled price, consumers are just unable to pay as much as they would wish, and this problem brings with it a variety of consequences in its train.

These relatively scarce goods have to be allocated finally, and as the price mechanism is incapable of performing this task, other methods have to be found. It might be that sellers will sell to the first customers who arrive, or suppliers might only sell to their favourite customers. The government might instal a system of rationing so that a sense of fairness appears. Under these circumstances a 'black market' will tend to emerge, where the price controls are evaded, and the goods sold illegally at more than the maximum price. Consumers, if given the opportunity, would be willing to pay OP^2 for the restricted supply on OM^1, but this destroys the original intention of the price control which was to keep the price below the equilibrium price for the benefit of the mass of consumers. An attempt to keep prices low has merely resulted in an artificial shortage of the good.

To avoid this shortage, governments can supplement this price control by agreeing to grant a subsidy to producers. Producers will only produce what the consumers are demanding at the controlled price if they themselves receive sufficient revenue. Figure 1 would indicate that producers must receive a price of OP^2 per unit for the good, for a level of output of OM to be produced, and so a subsidy of P^1P^2 would have to be paid for this output to emerge.

There are price controls which will not lead to shortages of a product. This was illustrated when the previous existence of resale price maintenance gave the manufacturer power to prevent the retailer from selling goods below prescribed prices. The idea can be seen also in the labour market when the government introduces minimum wage legislation. In Fig. 2 below assume that labour is homogeneous with DD and SS representing the demand for and supply of labour respectively. The equilibrium wage would be OP with OM people being employed. If the government felt that this wage was too low and decided to legislate that no one must pay a wage less than OP^1, then employers would only want to employ OM^1 units of labour even though the labour force offering themselves for work would have increased to OM^2.

Instead of a scarcity of labour occurring after government intervention, there is a distinct surplus of the product, labour. In fact, as only OM^1 will

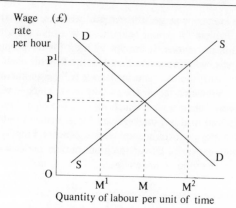

Fig. 2

be employed, the result has been an increase in unemployment, i.e. M¹M. The government's good intentions may well have resulted in helping to raise the wage of some people, but nevertheless the overall effect will be a surplus of labour looking for employment. No black market is likely to exist but there is ample evidence that some workers will offer to work for wages below the legally prescribed level.

Comments

A. Specific points

1. Division of the essay into **three** sections:

   a. Explain how a free market economy allows the price mechanism to resolve the scarcity problem—this should be brief and to the point.

   b. Explain how maximum price legislation results in artificial shortage.

   c. Explain how minimum price legislation results in a surplus.

   Sections **b.** and **c.** should be given an equal status.

2. Points of Emphasis:

   a. The allocative powers of the price mechanism are convincingly demonstrated in free market economies. Positions of excess demand and excess supply are made to disappear by allowing the price mechanism free movement.

   b. The attempt by governments to solve one problem merely leads to the creation of another. Interfering with the price mechanism, even with the best of motives, will cause a shortage of a good. The 'invisible hand' of the price mechanism is not allowed to function, and other allocative measures are called for, which tend to result in an inequitable state of affairs.

   c. Not all government price legislation leads to scarcity—some legislation may lead to a position of surplus instead. An example of minimum price control must be introduced such as minimum wage levels. The government might be acting with the very best intentions to assist lower paid workers, but that action will merely result in the demand for labour being much less than the supply of that labour being offered in the market. It may be all right for the people who are still employed at this higher wage, but that does not help the unemployed very much. The relative elasticity of demand for labour will be an important factor in the government intervention, as an elastic demand for labour will mean a greater number of people unemployed, which may be too high a price to pay for the existence of a well paid but smaller work force. It might saddle the government with enormous payments of unemployment benefits. Employers might decide to carry this more expensive labour force but only at the cost of passing on the extra wages in the form of price rises.

B. General Points

1. Make sure you understand the following terms:

a. *ad valorem* tax	**d.** resale price maintenance
b. deficiency payment	**e.** cobweb theory
c. rationing	**f.** black market.

2. Why are prices so important?

    a. The usual answer given would be that it is a key factor in the cost of living, but a more fundamental answer an economist might offer would be that it assists in the optimal allocation of scarce resources. The movement of prices will result in factors of production taking up their most productive uses, and society will finally obtain maximum satisfaction from the use of these resources. The constant competition will result in an efficiently organised economy.

    b. Prices should reflect the manner in which society values things; prices should also reflect the scarcity and so the cost of bringing these items to the market. But in the real world of consumer ignorance and monopoly power, prices may diverge from this idealised state of reflecting our wants and the cost of meeting them. It is in these circumstances that the government feels bound to manipulate the price mechanism for both social and political ends.

    c. Governments have intervened in the free functioning of the price mechanism in a number of ways:

        i. maximum and minimum price legislation
        ii. introduction of indirect taxation or subsidies
        iii. schemes to provide stability in prices and incomes (usually in agriculture).

3. What happens to the price of a good when an indirect tax is imposed?

    The government might impose an indirect tax on a good—although strictly speaking it is really imposing the tax on the person selling the good. The full burden of the tax may fall on the producer or the consumer, much depending on the concept of elasticity.

The tax might be 'specific' (or so much per unit sold) or *ad valorem* (or a certain proportion of the value of the good). The expenditure tax would result in raising the costs of the supplier and thus his supply curve would be decreased and shifted to the left by the amount of the tax. If the tax was of the 'specific' variety, the new supply curve would be drawn parallel to the original one.

Remember that the introduction of such a tax would not alter the position of the demand curve facing the supplier, and so the final equilibrium price would be dependent on the combination of the demand and supply elasticities.

In Fig. 3 DD and SS represent the demand and supply of a particular good with the equilibrium price being OP. A tax increase would shift the supply curve upwards and to the left by an amount equal to NR. But if the supplier tried to pass on the entire tax increase and charge OP^1 the consumers would only demand OM^1. The supplier is forced to charge a price of OP^2 and sell OM^2 which means that both he and the consumers are sharing the burden of the tax—or incidence. The total amount of tax taken by the Chancellor is $OM^2 \times PP^1$, i.e. the number of units sold multiplied by the rate of tax per unit.

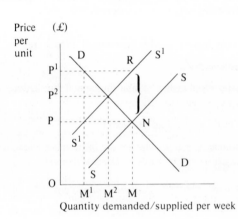

Fig. 3

Essay questions

1. *It has been advocated that the government should introduce a minimum wage for all wage earners while at the same time producers should set a price ceiling on the goods they sell to consumers. What are likely to be the effects of such a policy?* (JMB)

2. *Discuss briefly why it might be thought desirable to stabilise the prices of primary products. Analyse the various way in which a greater degree of such price stability might be achieved.* (Lond.)

3. *Analyse critically alternative methods of ensuring a minimum income for farmers.* (Oxf.)

4. *A government decides that it desires to raise the incomes of farmers producing a certain foodstuff. Using demand and supply curves illustrate the consequences of each of the following alternative policies.*

   a. *Directives to farmers to restrict crop acreages.*

   b. *Intervention purchases of the crop by the government to achieve a certain price in the market.*

   c. *A system of deficiency payments whereby the government pays farmers an amount per unit equal to the difference between the free market price and a guaranteed price, if the former is lower than the latter. (WJEC)*

Brief comments on essay questions

Question 2

The question distinctly mentions the word 'briefly' in the first section. Candidates should respond by concentrating on the essentials.

1. Primary products (as represented by agricultural goods) are:

   a. goods of inelastic demand

   b. goods of inelastic supply (they exhibit unplanned fluctuations in production).

   These combined characteristics involve prices fluctuating more than for manufactured goods, and leads to the dual problem of

   a. fluctuating incomes

   b. lower than average incomes.

   The problem is seen more clearly in underdeveloped countries which rely so heavily on revenue gained from selling primary products.

2. The uncertainty element in production of agricultural products will allow prices to fluctuate between a certain range. These prices can be kept fairly stable if a cartel of producers agreed to limit production coming on to the market—with the proviso that excess stock should be stored or a deficiency of stock be released on to the market from previously held stocks.

   Government action can achieve the same result but any continual storing up of crops will have to be dealt with by destroying them, 'dumping' them overseas or just giving them away—each method of relief is faced with its own difficulty.

   Governments may offer guaranteed prices to farmers, and be prepared to pay the difference in the form of a deficiency payment should the market price be less than the guaranteed price.

   A more modern example of cartel operation can be seen in the OPEC system where agreements to restrict output and raise prices have resulted in a tremendous growth in the revenues of the oil exporters. It seems that a primary product which is in inelastic supply and inelastic demand has much to offer its fortunate producers.

Suggestions for further reading

Hewitt, G. *Economics of the Market.* (Fontana/Collins, 1971.) Chapter 2
Lipsey, R. G. *An Introduction to Positive Economics.* (Weidenfeld & Nicolson, 1975.) Chapter 11
Powicke, J. C. *Economic Theory.* (Arnold, 1968.) Chapter 12
Perrow, J. A. *Economics.* (University Tutorial Press Ltd, 1971) Chapter 6
Stanlake, G. F. *Introductory Economics.* (Longman, 1974.) Chapter 14

Essay number 7

Distinguish between the fixed and variable costs of a firm, and explain their significance for the firm's output decisions.   (O/C Board)

Suggested answer

Firms use different factors of production in producing their outputs and these particular inputs can themselves be categorised into fixed and variable factors.

Fixed costs, sometimes called overheads, are the costs incurred when purchasing indivisible factors, such as buildings, machinery, etc. But even if they are not used to produce any output at all, they have already been purchased and therefore incur fixed costs. Output may go up or down but these costs remain fixed. Further examples can be given in the form of rent, rates and depreciation of machinery, etc.

Variable costs on the other hand, are the costs paid by a firm in purchasing such items as labour and raw materials in the task of producing more output. In the short run, when the firm cannot change its fixed factors or capacity, i.e. it cannot extend its factory, the only way to increase output is by purchasing more variable factors. These variable costs, sometimes known as direct costs, change as output changes.

Every firm will have some combination of fixed and variable costs, and together their summation will indicate the total costs of the firm. When a firm is faced by changed market conditions in the form of increased demand for its product, the existence of that combination of fixed and variable costs looms large, and will undoubtedly affect the decision-making process of that firm.

In the first place, the time factor plays an important role in output decisions, and economists often regard the short period as a period of time when some factors are fixed and it is impossible to alter the capacity. Under these circumstances the only method of expanding output would be

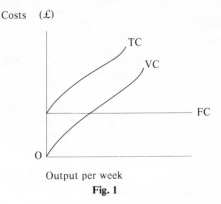

Costs (£)

Fig. 1

Output per week

by increasing the other variable inputs. One can see from Fig. 1 that fixed costs are constant and that when output is small these fixed costs will be spread over a very few units, resulting in high average costs. It is essential therefore for sufficient output to be produced, so that every unit carries a smaller proportion of fixed cost. Although average costs may fall in the early stages as the firm's capacity is better utilised, inevitably the law of diminishing returns will be encountered, resulting in rising average costs as the firm's capacity is pushed gradually to the limit. In the long period, the capacity of the firm may be altered, and thus all costs may be regarded as variable, so that these factors can be combined in the best possible way. Supply can then adjust completely to the new change in demand.

The significance of fixed and variable costs can also be appreciated when the firm must decide whether or not to continue producing after a fall in demand. The entrepreneur will have already incurred the expense of buying fixed-capital equipment and so even if production were completely stopped he will not be saving anything in the fixed-cost area. The expression 'bygones are forever bygones' is an appropriate phrase here because the entrepreneur cannot regain the money previously spent on these items. One could even say that the opportunity cost of using them was zero, especially if we assume that they have no alternative use. He is therefore left to contemplate on whether he can cover his variable costs by incoming revenue when producing. If this is the case, production may well continue as the difference between his receipts and variable costs would help towards paying off some of the fixed costs.

This could be shown in diagram form (see Fig. 2) where the firm will still continue to produce output OQ even though it is not covering all its costs. The firm is making a loss but continues to produce in the short run as long as it covers its variable costs. This perfectly competitive firm will try to maximise its profits, or in this case, minimise its losses. It will produce at a level where its MR is equal to its MC and it is at this point that its AR is covering its AVC, but not its ATC. Its total revenue at this level of output is OPNQ, but its total costs are OSMQ. It could not continue with this state of affairs in the long run, as profits have to be made eventually.

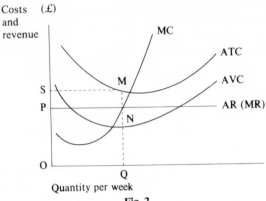

Fig. 2

In the long run, the firm may be able to take advantage of some of the economies of scale, and given sufficient time, may be able to adjust the size of plant so that it will be able to operate at the lowest possible average cost.

Comments

A. Specific points

1. Division of the essay into **two** sections:

   a. An introductory section defining fixed and variable costs—not more than a paragraph or two.

   b. A main section containing *two* elements of importance:
      i. The impending effect of diminishing returns in the short run, followed by the possible economies of scale in the long run
      ii. The decision whether or not to produce in the short run, knowing that fixed costs cannot be covered.

   A case can be made for concentrating on either **i.** or **ii.**, and not both, but this essay contains *both* parts even though they are therefore covered somewhat superficially.

2. Points of Emphasis:

   a. The question revolves around the time interval during which production is carried out. The short and long run must be introduced and defined.

   b. The use made of the fixed capacity in terms of variable factors will result in either an underutilisation or overutilisation of the fixed factor, leading to changes in the average and marginal product.

   c. The inevitability of diminishing returns in the short run may encourage firms to adjust their capacity so that in the long run the correct capacity can be adopted according to the level of output required.

   d. 'Bygones are forever bygones' must be a standard by which firms' decisions are judged. Even though fixed costs (which are bygones) cannot be covered, the criterion of covering the variable costs in the short run is paramount.

3. Differing Interpretations:

This particular essay could be attacked in a number of ways:

a. the manner outlined in the essay.

b. an all out account of the effect of the law of diminishing returns, followed by the economies of scale, on the output decisions of the entrepreneur.

c. a more detailed analysis of the short run and long run positions of the firm when a change in the level of demand involves a coverage of average variable costs but not average total costs. This would entail showing a detailed knowledge of interrelationships between the various costs, such as MC, AC, AFC, and AVC.

B. General points

1. Can you *draw* cost curves and do you *understand the relationship* between the cost curves themselves? Can you *calculate* costs from a table?

Drawing Cost Curves (Fig. 3)

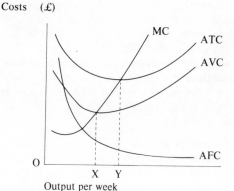

Fig. 3

a. Always label the curves
b. Always label the axes of the graph
c. MC must cut ATC and AVC at their minimum points
d. AVC can never be above ATC
e. AFC must continually slope downwards to the right

Understanding Relationships

a. ATC is made up of two components—AFC and AVC.
b. Why does ATC fall over a certain range of output and yet AVC is rising? Between OX and OY, the rise in AVC is outweighed by the rate of fall in AFC. What happens after output OY?

c. Why can ATC fall when MC is rising?
The answer lies *not* in whether MC is rising or falling, but the level of MC in relation to ATC. As long as MC is less than the existing ATC it will force down the
ATC. As long as a cricketer's current innings is less than his previous average,
the new average must fall.

Calculating Costs

a. TFC + TVC = TC

b. $\dfrac{TC}{output} = ATC = AVC + AFC$

c. $\dfrac{TVC}{output} = AVC$

d. $\dfrac{TFC}{output} = AFC$

e. $\dfrac{\Delta TC}{\Delta output} = MC$ (change in output by one unit)

f. $TC_n - TC_{n-1} = MC_n$

2. Points essential to understand

- **a.** What have 'diminishing returns' and 'decreasing returns' in common? They are
  often used synonomously to mean a decrease in the marginal product. But it is
  important to realise what *causes* the marginal product to fall. With diminishing
  returns, the marginal product falls due to an overutilisation of a fixed capacity,
  or in other words, changing proportions of fixed to variable factors. In the latter
  case, the advantages of size have been overshadowed by the diseconomies of
  scale resulting in the marginal product falling. Whatever term is used it is advisable to qualify it, e.g. increasing returns due to scale or diminishing returns
  due to changing proportions.

- **b.** What does the term 'returns' mean?
  The laws of returns (for whatever reason) are fundamentally involved in the
  physical yield. Returns do not mean money in this case, but physical units of
  production.

- **c.** When do diseconomies of scale begin?
  The usual diagram portraying economies and diseconomies of scale gives the impression that at a particular level of output, the advantages of size terminate and
  the disadvantages of size begin. In actual fact, as scale increases a firm will
  experience both advantages and disadvantages of size, but the former is usually
  dominating the latter to such an extent that average costs continue to fall. When
  average costs begin to rise after capacity has reached a certain size, one can say
  that the prevalent diseconomies of scale have begun to outweigh the correspon-
  ding economies of scale.

- **d.** Is a firm most profitable when it is most efficient?
  When a firm is operating efficiently, i.e. at the minimum point of its AC curve, it
  is said to be producing an optimum output. But a most profitable level of output
  involves marginal decisions with the attempt to equate MC and MR. Even then

there is no guarantee as the position achieved might be a least loss position. An optimum output level and a most profitable output level can be one and the same when the price, marginal revenue, marginal cost and average cost are all equal. This is the long run equilibrium position of a perfectly competitive firm.

Essay questions

1. *If a competitive firm's average cost exceeds its average revenue should it remain in business? Anyalyse the problem in terms of the short run time period and the long run time period. (CA)*

2. *Define the law of diminishing returns. What arguments would you use to convince a sceptic of the validity of such a law? (IB)*

3. *Distinguish between 'diminishing returns' and 'diseconomies of scale'. (Lond.)*

4. *Why would an entrepreneur distinguish between the short and the long run when faced with a change in market conditions? (O/C Board)*

5. *'A reduction in demand raises firms' costs of production per unit of output and so leads to increases in prices'.   Discuss. (Oxf.)*

6. *Discuss the reasons why the long run average costs of firms producing certain commodities may fall over certain ranges of output as output is increased. (WJEC)*

Brief comments on essay questions

Question 2

Candidates must keep the first section as *brief* as possible. All that is required is:

a. Simple definition ('as we add successive units of one factor to fixed amounts of other factors, the increments in total output will at first rise and then decline').
b. A diagram illustrating the marginal and average product curves showing one curve starting to fall before the other begins to fall.
c. A statistical table including fixed and variable factors combining to give a total product, which will finally increase at a decreasing rate.

The arguments used depend upon the following statements being correct:

i. factors of production are scarce;
ii. factors of production are poor substitutes for each other;
iii. factors of production are very immobile and not easily adaptable.

These statements form the basis of 'the law':

i. Fertile land or easily accessible coal seams are scarce, and any increase in production in association with either factor will result in more marginal land being used or more inaccessible seams being negotiated, all of which will lead to a greater output but at a greatly increased cost.

ii. When factors are combined in certain proportions to produce a level of output, any further output can only be forthcoming after an increase in one of these factors which might be substituted for another. But as factors are imperfect substitutes for each other, any movement from the optimum combination of factors would necessarily lead to greater costs. If this were not so, all the food the world required could be produced by merely increasing the units of labour working on a single piece of land.

iii. Even labour which is in demand cannot easily be made adaptable to the work required of it, if it has had to leave a completely different way of life.

A living proof of the existence of such a law is the poverty and degradation of the combination of increasing population in an underdeveloped country.

Suggestions for further reading

Giles, C. ed., *Understanding Economics*. (The Manchester Economics Project—Ginn & Co, 1971.) Chapters 9–11

Harvey, J. *Modern Economics*. (Macmillan, 1974.) Chapters 10–11

Lipsey, R. G. *An Introduction to Positive Economics*. (Weidenfeld & Nicolson, 1975.) Chapter 18

Livesey, F. *A Textbook of Economics*. (Polytech Publishers Ltd, 1978.) Chapter 24

Marshall, B. V. *Comprehensive Economics: Part 2*. (Longman, 1974.) Chapter 10

Whitehead, G. *Economics Made Simple*. (W. H. Allen, 1974.) Chapters 5, 8

Stanlake, G. F. *Introductory Economics*. (Longman, 1971.) Chapters 5–7

An appendix

Two vital decisions to be made by a firm

a. How to make the best use of the firm's capacity, i.e. how to be efficient in the short run.

b. How to produce a given rate of output most efficiently, i.e. how to choose that combination of factors of production which will enable the firm to produce a given output at the minimum average cost—in the long run.

a. *Decision Number 1*

  i. The firm is operating *in the short run*, when the firm's capacity is assumed to be fixed and incapable of change.

  ii. Increased production can only arise from the addition of variable factors such as labour and materials. This changes the proportions in which fixed and variable factors are combined.

  iii. The inputs will yield physical returns in the shape of products and total product will rise, quickly at first and then more slowly. The law of variable proportions is seen to be operating whereby marginal and average product rises at first to be followed by a decline first in marginal product and then average product. The fundamental reason for this movement is that initially the fixed factor is underutilised and then becomes overutilised.

iv. A firm will tend to experience increasing returns, constant returns, and finally diminishing returns—all due to the effect of changing proportions of the fixed to variable factors.

v. The entrepreneur will have reached a *technical efficiency* within the firm when the ratio of fixed to variable factors gives him the maximum average product. It may be regarded as the *technical optimum level of output*, but is certainly not the most profitable level of output since costs and revenues have yet to be considered.

vi. *Economic efficiency* can only be achieved from a knowledge of the inputs' physical yield and the inputs' price. Economic and technical data are necessary to produce the firm's cost structure. Assuming that the entrepreneur faces perfectly elastic supply curves for all factors of production i.e. he accepts the market prices of the factors as given, and can purchase as much as he likes without altering their prices, then any cost changes must stem from changes in productivity.

vii. Additional variable factors will expand output and cause total costs to rise, but average and marginal cost curves will tend to be U shaped. The marginal cost is the cost of producing an extra unit of output. As extra men are employed the extra output obtained increases, and as the cost of employing an extra man remains the same, the marginal cost will be falling. As the law of diminishing returns takes effect, the marginal product per man falls, bringing with it a rise in the marginal cost.

viii. The average cost curve is also U shaped. In the early stages, average cost will be high when output is small, but as output increases the fixed costs are spread over more units of production, causing average cost to fall. When diminishing returns set in, the fixed factor becomes overutilised, resulting in rising average cost.

ix. The entrepreneur will feel he is utilising his capacity most efficiently when he is producing an output at the minimum average cost. He is now economically efficient, i.e. an *economic optimum*. But don't forget that we are still considering the short-run picture.

In Fig. 4 it can be seen that OT is the technically optimum level of output, with diminishing returns setting in after point OD.

However, the firm is only in an economically optimum position when it is producing at the minimum average cost, which is indicated on the cost/output diagram (Fig. 5) by output level OX.

It is very important to remember that this position is *not necessarily* the most profitable position, as the revenue conditions have yet to be considered.

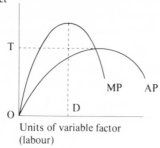

Product

T

O

D

MP   AP

Units of variable factor
(labour)

Fig. 4

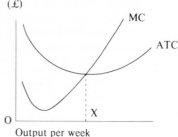

Cost (£)
per
unit

MC

ATC

O   X

Output per week

Fig. 5

b. *Decision Number 2*

i. *In the long run*, it is possible to vary *all* factors i.e. scale of production. A given output level can be produced by a number of different methods, and while increasing the scale of operations the entrepreneur may still keep the factor proportions unchanged.

ii. The increased size may allow the firm to experience (a) economies of scale i.e. increasing returns, with output increasing more than proportionately to the increase in the size of firm, and (b) diseconomies of scale i.e. decreasing returns, with output increasing less than proportionately to the increase in the size of firm.

iii. With factor prices remaining constant, the increased scale will reduce unit costs, the origin of which is the rate of increase in output. Finally costs per unit will rise when diseconomies of scale set in.

iv. *For every output level* there is a particular plant size giving the least cost method. Given time to adjust capacity, any level of output can be produced most cheaply. The line which joins all these minimum cost points is the long run average cost curve for the firm. It is impossible to produce these output levels at lower cost, unless there is a change in the prices of the factors of production, in which case less expensive factors will be substituted for more expensive factors, allowing a different long run average cost curve to emerge.

v. At any moment in time, a firm will be utilising its given capacity and presumably trying to utilise it most efficiently i.e. at the minimum point on the short run average cost curve. But this particular level of output could be produced at a lower unit cost if capacity could be increased. So in the short run, the firm would produce output OX at an average cost OC. In the long run, it could produce this output at a lower average cost OC^1 by operating within a bigger capacity. This can be illustrated on the diagram (Fig. 6) below containing three short-run average cost curves. The new short-run average cost curve associated with this larger capacity is $SRAC^2$, and it is seen that while it is producing OX more cheaply it is still not utilising the larger capacity most efficiently. Although not drawing them on the diagram, there will be a separate SRAC curve for each different level of output i.e. for every capacity level. It would obviously pay a

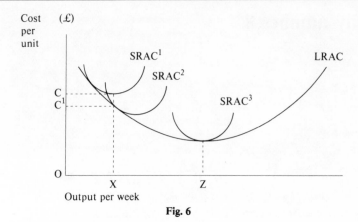

Fig. 6

firm to build a plant appropriate to a given rate of output even it if means underutilising that particular capacity. Given the firm's LRAC curve, there is only one level of output which can be produced from the firm's capacity enabling the firm to produce that output most efficiently and at the same time utilising that capacity most efficiently i.e. OZ. It is only in this case where the minimum point on the SRAC curve forms a tangent to the LRAC curve.

vi. It is only when output is at OZ that the firm will be of *optimum* size, i.e. when it is making the most efficient use of the resources it employs, *and* be producing at the lowest possible cost.

Essay number 8

Distinguish between the equilibrium of the firm and of the industry under conditions of perfect competition.   (O/C Board)

Suggested answer

Firms are constantly changing their price and output decisions in relation to their cost and revenue structures. Their behaviour will depend to a great extent upon the particular market form in which they find themselves. Even so we can make the general assumption that firms are trying to achieve a level of output which maximises their profits, irrespective of this particular market form.

There are many limiting conditions when a firm finds itself in a situation of 'perfect competition'. They range from supplying an homogeneous product, having perfect knowledge of the prices and profits pertaining in the market, to a perfect mobility of all types of factors in different uses and availability to everyone. But perhaps one of the most important assumptions must be that there are a large number of buyers and sellers who control such a minute part of the market that their influence on the market price is nil. They can be said to be price takers, who can offer for sale any quantity they wish at the ruling market price, over which they have no control. The competitive nature of this situation will also call for the existence of free entry into or exit from the market, a condition which is essential when the signalling nature of profits persuades other firms to attempt to reap some of the rewards achieved by an industry.

Once the firm has achieved maximum profit there will be no incentive for it to change its output level and equilibrium will have been reached. The firm will have control over its costs but it must appreciate that the price at which it will sell all its units has been determined for it by market forces. There is no point in raising the price as no one will buy from it considering the perfect knowledge which exists, and one would be unlikely to lower the price when one can sell as much as one wants at the ruling market price. One can state that the firm is faced by a perfectly elastic demand for its product.

The firm will be attempting to produce a level of output where the cost of making another unit is equal to the revenue received from selling that unit. Thus when MC equals MR this will be a profit maximising position, and it follows that as in perfect competition marginal revenue is the same as price, a firm must try to equate MC with price. This can be shown in Fig. 1 where the firm's maximum profit (equilibrium) position is OQ, i.e. where price (MR) equals MC. Abnormal profit is being earned at OQ and can be represented by the rectangle RPTS. The firm has reached a position of short run equilibrium.

There are in fact two other short-run equilibrium positions for firms to achieve. These are (Figs. 2 and 3) where the price just covers average cost, i.e. a position of normal profits, and where the price fails to cover AC but more than covers AVC, a position of minimum loss.

However the industry is not in equilibrium as it can only reach this state when there is no tendency for the number of firms or the output to change.

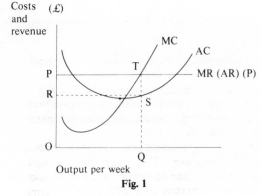

Fig. 1

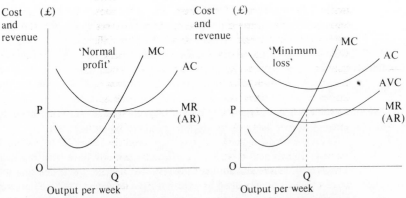

Fig. 2   Fig. 3

The assumption of free entry to the industry of new producers immediately transforms the situation of abnormal profits made by firms as shown in the first diagram by the rectangle PRTS. Not only will new firms enter in order to try to gain some of the rewards, but existing firms will attempt to expand their capacities in order to lower their average costs (gaining the economies of scale). The expansion of output all round will shift the market supply curve to the right forcing the market price down until the abnormal profits disappear. Only when firms are making normal profits (that level of profit which makes it just worthwhile to stay in the present line of production) will there be no incentive for new firms to enter the industry. There will be a continual attempt for firms to achieve their optimum size (most efficient), and in the long run, this would be at the minimum point of their individual long-run average cost curve. It is only at that point that they will have exploited any further economies of scale within their grasp. This is shown in Fig. 4 where firms will be operating at output level OQ, and as in perfect competition all firms have the same technology available, then all their cost curves will be identical.

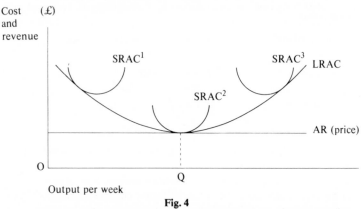

Fig. 4

At this stage all the firms in the industry are maximising their profits (MC = P); all firms are making normal profits (AR = AC); and all firms are producing at the minimum point on their long run AC curves (AR = MR = MC = AC). The industry is in long-run equilibrium.

Comments

A. Specific points

1. Division of the essay into **three** sections:

   a. Definition and assumptions of perfect competition—this is merely introductory and should not exceed a paragraph in length.

   b. Equilibrium position of firms in the short run.

   c. Equilibrium positions of industry in the long run.

   Sections **b.** and **c.** must form the major part of the essay.

2. Points of Emphasis:

   a. The two main assumptions of perfect competition are:
   - **i.** firms are price takers
   - **ii.** no restriction of entry.

   b. The equilibrium position of a firm is the most profitable position, and is that output where MR = MC. It could signify a minimum loss position as well.

   c. Equilibrium for an industry is when the number of firms is constant, showing no tendency to change. Perhaps it is wrong to speak of the short run equilibrium position of the industry, as profit signals old and new firms to expand, thereby increasing supply. The falling price rearranges the profit status of firms, until normal profits occur.

   d. In the final analysis, firms end up in a maximum profit yet normal profit position, with optimum positions achieved. Efficiency has been achieved and the consumer can feel well pleased.

B. General points

1. Make sure you understand the following terms:

a. a firm's demand curve	**d.** normal profit
b. equilibrium output	**e.** abnormal profit
c. optimum output	**f.** market demand.

2. The following points are often confused by candidates:

   a. *Why is the market demand curve and the perfectly competitive firm's demand curve different but related?*
   The market price in a perfectly competitive industry is determined by the forces of supply and demand. The industry's supply curve is made up of the outputs of individual firms, and this is linked with the market demand curve, i.e. the willingness of consumers to buy the good at a series of different prices. The final market price must be accepted by each firm in the knowledge that it cannot be changed by that firm—or any firm acting individually, i.e. the demand curve facing the industry is downward sloping to the right—the market demand curve. But the demand curve facing each individual firm is horizontal—the firm's demand curve is perfectly elastic.

   Although an individual firm doesn't have enough influence to affect the market price, a concerted action by all the firms will force the market supply curve to shift to the left or right, thereby changing the market price. In fact, the action by all the firms in expanding output tends to be detrimental to them in that the result is a fall in price and less profit earned.

   It is usual to place the two diagrams (Figs. 5 and 6) alongside each other in order to indicate the level of market price which individual firms have to accept. But what is not so obvious is that while the vertical scale is identical the horizontal scales cannot be so. The quantity supplied by the firm is OQ and this must be a very small proportion of the amount supplied by the industry, i.e. OZ.

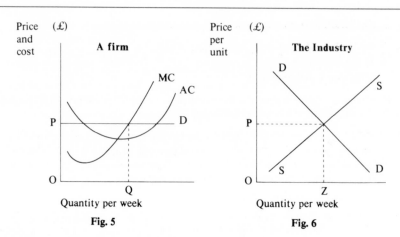

Fig. 5   Fig. 6

b. *When is 'marginal revenue' identical to 'average revenue'?*
Whatever the market conditions, price and average revenue must be the same, but marginal and average revenue are only the same when average revenue is constant. This can be illustrated by the following table:

Price (£)	Number of Units Sold	Total Revenue (£)	Average Revenue (£)	Marginal Revenue (£)	
5	1	5	5	—	TR = unit sold × price
4	2	8	4	3	AR = TR ÷ units sold
3	3	9	3	1	MR = change in TR brought about
2	5	10	2	$\frac{1}{2}$	by the sale of an extra
1	8	8	1	$\frac{2}{3}$	unit.

The data given above indicate a downward sloping demand curve (as seen in imperfect competition). In this case MR will always be below AR because in order to sell more of the good the price of all units of the good has to be reduced. For instance, to sell 3 units the price must be reduced to £3, but the MR is not £3 because the price has to be reduced on the previous 2 units. There is a gain of £3 by selling the third unit, but a loss of £1 each on the other 2 units, making in total a gain of only £1.

If the above table had a constant price level at say £5, calculations would show that both AR and MR would be the same as price—make sure that you can agree with this!

c. *Is equilibrium any different within different market conditions?*
Assuming firms are attempting to maximise profits, firms will try to make the gap between total revenue and total costs as large as possible. When a firm increases output by an extra unit and adds more to revenue than costs, profits will be increasing. It follows that a firm will keep increasing output until the increase in revenue is identical to the increase in costs, i.e. where MR = MC. This statement applies to firms operating under *any* market conditions—not just perfect competition.

The equilibrium position requires a qualification in that:

i. in the short tun AR must be covering AVC
ii. in the long run AR must be covering ATC (in fact in the long run in perfect competition AR will be equal to ATC).

3. Can you visualise a perfectly competitive industry?

a. *In the short run?* Imagine an industry composed of a large number of small firms, each firm having an identical cost curve. They all face the same price and they all equate this price (MR) to MC. They are all in equilibrium but the level of profit they make is one or other of the following:

i. abnormal profit: AR > AC
ii. normal profit; AR = AC
iii. minimum losses: AR < AC (but AR > AVC).
The firms are all making the same profit or the same losses.

b. *In the long run?* Imagine an industry of small firms all making abnormal profits. The existence of these profits will:
i. persuade new firms to enter this industry.
ii. persuade existing firms to expand their capacity.
In both instances, the effect on the supply of the good will be to shift the market supply curve to the right, thereby forcing the market price downwards.
There are two forces set in motion

i. the price of the product is forced in a downward direction.
ii. each firm, new and old, will try to increase capacity and obtain previously-unexploited economies of scale. This will continue until it achieves the optimum size plant. This is where the firm's short-run average cost curve and its long-run average cost curve form a tangent at the former's minimum point. These two forces will come to a halt when there are not more abnormal profits to be obtained i.e. when the price cuts the firm's cost curve at its minimum point. Normal profits are being obtained by each firm and the industry is in a state of equilibrium.

4. Why is the study of perfect competition so important?

Each firm in the long run will be:

a. maximising its profits (producing where MR = MC)
b. making normal profits (producing where AR = AC)
c. making optimum output (producing where AC is at a minimum).

The outstanding feature of perfect competition is that price is always equal to marginal cost, and this in itself brings about an ideal allocation of resources. Price is always equal to marginal cost in perfect competition because a firm tries to maximise profits by equating MR and MC. Since MR is equal to AR in perfect competition, AR is equal to MC i.e. price equals MC. In any other market conditions, equilibrium positions are obtained with price being greater than MC, and it is this which suggests that an optimal allocation of resources is absent.

A consumer will buy a commodity until the marginal utility from that commodity is equal to its price. The price of the good indicates the money value the consumer places on the marginal unit. A producer will find that his resources are scarce and the marginal cost of production measures the extent to which resources are used by the last unit of the good which is produced. When price equals marginal cost, society is placing a value on the last unit it buys which is equal to the loss in the form of resources used up in the production of that last unit. But if price exceeds marginal cost, society is suggesting that it values the marginal unit more than the cost of producing it in terms of resources lost. The output level is too low and further resources are used up in producing more, so that society has allocated its resources in an optimal fashion.

5. Is the normal assumption too hypothetical?

Most textbooks will assume that all firms are identical, but if we assume that firms differ, a structure of high and low cost firms will appear. Equilibrium will exist in this set of circumstances when the least efficient firm is making 'normal profits'. Firms making these 'normal profits' may be considered 'marginal firms'. They are the first to leave the industry if there is a reduction in demand leading to a fall in price.

Essay questions

1. *What characteristics must a market possess to be described as perfect? Is there any market in the real world which possesses these characteristics?* *(IB)*
2. *'A firm maximises profits when marginal costs equal average costs.' Comment.* *(Lond.)*
3. *Analyse the equilibrium of the firm and the industry in both perfect and imperfect competition.* *(O/C Board)*
4. *'The optimum allocation of resources would be achieved were prices to be set equal to marginal production costs for all products.' Discuss.* *(O/C Board)*
5. *'Under perfect competition, only normal profits are earned.' Discuss.* *(Oxf.)*
6. *Explain what the term 'competition' means to the economist and to the businessman. Why, on the whole, do you think that Western Governments regard competition as economically desirable?* *(JMB)*

Brief comments on essay questions

Question 2

Many essay questions are framed in the form of a statement to be commented upon. Candidates find it difficult to know where and how to begin with this type of question. Most of these statements contain an element of truth under certain circumstances, and good answers will show when the statement is valid followed by an explanation when circumstances make the statement invalid.

Suggested format

1. Introduction:

   a. How does a firm maximise profits?
   It produces a level of output up to the point where marginal revenue equals marginal costs. This equilibrium condition applies under any market conditions.

   b. How do a firm's marginal costs relate to its average costs?
   A firm's marginal costs will always cut its average costs at the minimum point on the average cost curve.

   c. The statement is implying that the firm will always maximise its profits when it produces an output at the minimum point of its average cost curve, i.e. an optimum output.

2. Perfect Competition:

   a. A firm can maximise its profits in the short run, showing an abnormal profit position—where marginal cost is above average cost (illustrate with a diagram).

   b. A firm can maximise its profits in the long run, but only normal profit will be earned. The average revenue (marginal revenue) will be forced down until it forms a tangent to the average cost curve. The firm will be producing at the minimum point on its average cost curve (illustrate with a diagram).

3. Monopoly:

   The short- and long-run position of a monopolist may be similar in that abnormal profits may be earned even in the long run. In this case marginal cost will be below average cost, and production will take place at a lower level than the optimum (illustrate with a diagram).

Suggestions for further reading

Cairncross, A. K. *Introduction to Economics*. (Butterworth, 1973.) Chapters 16–17

Giles, C., ed. *Understanding Economics*. (Manchester Project—Ginn & Co., 1971.) Chapter 11

Harvey, J. *Modern Economics*. (Macmillan, 1974.) Chapters 11–12

Hewitt, G. *Economics of the Market*. (Fontana/Collins, 1971.) Chapter 8

Lipsey, R. G. *An Introduction to Positive Economics*. (Weidenfeld & Nicolson, 1975.) Chapter 20

Stanlake, G. F. *Introductory Economics* (Longman, 1971.) Chapter 15

Whitehead, G. *Economics Made Simple*. (W. H. Allen, 1974.) Chapter 9

Essay number 9

Will a profit maximising monopolist always benefit by increasing the price of his product?   (IB)

Suggested answer

Monopoly legislation in the UK defines a monopoly as a situation where a dominant seller controls one quarter of the market. Theoretically one tends to look on a monopolist as a sole seller or supplier in an industry. In fact as there is only one firm, it is the industry.

With this control over supply, the monopolist can easily influence the price. Any restriction of supply by the firm results in the market supply curve shifting to the left and forcing the price upwards. So the firm can fix the price; it is a price maker and not a price taker as in perfect competition. Even so, the firm still has to rely on the wishes of the consumers as to the quantity which will be demanded and therefore sold, at that higher price. The market demand curve facing the firm will be downward sloping to the right, indicating that if a high price is envisaged, then the consumers will demand less of the product. The monopolist firm could of course decide on the quantity that it wished to produce and sell but it would have to rely on the demand curve to see what price would have to be charged to clear the market. The monopolist cannot fix both the price and the quantity sold at the same time.

The monopolist will now attempt to fix a price or produce a level of output which will maximise his profits. To achieve this he will attempt to equate MR with MC, as at any point less than this, more will be added to his revenue than his costs, and profit could be increased by raising output. This can be illustrated by Fig. 1 where an output of OQ is produced selling at a price of OA per unit with an abnormal profit of ABCD being obtained. The MR curve facing the monopolist is not the same as the price

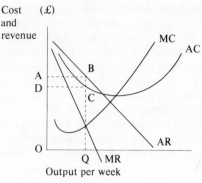

Fig. 1

(AR) curve. As the demand curve (AR) is downward sloping, the price of an extra unit has to be reduced in order for that unit to be sold. Not only must this extra unit be reduced in price, but all the previous units must be reduced in price also. The change in total revenue brought about by the sale of an extra unit, i.e. MR, will be less than the price received for that unit, giving a downward sloping MR curve which will be below the price (AR) curve at all points.

The monopolist is capable of increasing the price until his MR equals MC. He will then have maximised his profit, and there is no need for him to move from this position. Monopoly power is associated with inelastic demand in that even if the price is raised demand will not fall off appreciably. And yet we can say that a profit maximising monopolist will never sell at a price at which demand is inelastic because if he did, then he could raise his total revenue and reduce his total cost by actually selling less (or raising price). In fact, at that point, he would not be maximising his profit.

This can be illustrated by Fig. 2 where a monopolist would not attempt to produce an output greater than OM because any such output to the right of OM will imply a relatively inelastic demand. Marginal revenue at these output levels would be negative and so the monopolist could increase his total revenue and reduce total costs by reducing his output. We

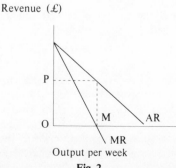

Fig. 2

can say then that a profit maximising monopolist would benefit by increasing the price of his product when demand is inelastic, but would
clearly be harmed if the price were raised when demand is elastic.

Consideration of non-theoretical arguments would mean that the power
of a monopolist to raise prices is always limited by the availability of close
substitutes. The existence of substitutes will make the demand curve more
elastic so that any small rise in price will have adverse effects on the total
revenue of the monopolist.

Charging an increased price may well stimulate rival producers to enter
the market and attempt to share in the potential profits. The high costs of
entering an industry may be inhibiting to potential producers, but the incentive of high profits may well persuade them to begin production.

Price increases may well lead trade unions to pressure their employers
for substantial wage claims. The profits earned by monopolists could well
encourage trade unions in getting their full share.

Finally, there is the ever present threat of government intervention if a
monopolist pushes his price to an unacceptable level.

Comments

A. Specific points

1. There is no clear cut division in this essay, only a series of interrelated points,
culminating in the concept of elasticity of demand.

2. Points of emphasis:

    a. Introductory comments on a monopolist including:
        i. definition
        ii. similarity between firm and industry
        iii. control over price
        iv. downward sloping demand curve.

    b. Equilibrium position of a monopolist—similar to perfect competition in that MR
= MC but there are differences, the main one being that P > MC.

    c. A full consideration of the connection between total revenue, the maximum
profit position and the elasticity of demand.

B. General points

1. Make sure you understand the following terms:

    a. monopsonist   **d.** negative marginal revenue
    b. monopoly profit   **e.** monopolist's demand curve
    c. discriminating monopolist   **f.** monopolist's supply curve.

2. Some essential truths:

a. Is the monopolist the industry?

Any change in the monopolist's output affects the market supply and thus the price. The ability to control the supply enables the monopolist to fix the price he can sell his output at, but he is at the mercy of the consumer as to how much they will purchase at that price. If he wants to produce and sell more he will be forced to do it at a lower price. He can fix his output level and even the price level, but the market demand is the force which decides how much he will *sell* at that price.

b. Is the firm's demand curve and the market demand curve the same?

The monopolist *is* faced by the market demand curve (AR) and it is downward sloping to the right. The associated marginal revenue curve will lie below it at all levels of output. The fundamental point to appreciate here is that although an extra unit may be sold at a lower price, the marginal revenue gained is *not* revenue coming in from the sale of that *particular* unit, because all the previous units have to be sold at that lower price involving a loss of revenue to the seller. The marginal revenue will be the gain in revenue from the sale of the last unit compared with the loss of revenue from selling previous units more cheaply. The final answer may be positive or negative. This can be illustrated by Fig. 3.

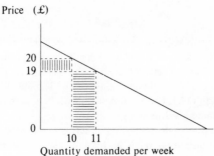

Fig. 3

If a monopolist is selling 10 units priced £20 each, and wants to sell one more, he is forced to lower his price to £19. The extra revenue obtained from selling the eleventh unit is £19 and is equal to the horizontally shaded rectangle. But the first ten units instead of selling at £20 each have to be sold at £19 each which is a loss of 10 units × £1 = £10. This is represented by the vertically shaded area.

Thus the real marginal revenue is the difference between the two areas or £19 − 10 = £9. This is obviously lower than the price when eleven units are sold.

c. Can monopoly profit remain for ever?

The short-run equilibrium position of the monopolist is where MR = MC. But this does not necessarily mean that the monopolist is making a profit. It is in the same situation exactly as the perfect competitor in that profit is only made if AR > AC. In the long run, the monopolist can maintain exactly the same position as in the short run with monopoly profit remaining intact (i.e. if AR was more than AC). But the attempt to maximise profit might result in the monopolist in-

creasing his scale and arriving at the appropriate sized plant for the level of demand. He has little control over demand but at least he may be able to reduce his
costs, thereby arriving at an even larger monopoly profit.

This can be illustrated on the diagram (Fig. 4) when the monopolist manages
to reduce his costs by increasing his capacity. His monopoly profit would initially be given by the area ABCD, which would be increased if the cost structure
could be lowered to AC^1.

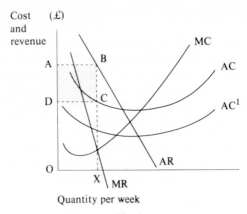

Fig. 4

d. Will a monopolist produce where demand is inelastic?

A monopolist's demand curve will vary in elasticity throughout its length
ranging from infinity to zero. Figure 5 (below) illustrates the changing values of
elasticity. At prices higher than OP elasticity of demand will be greater than 1; at
prices lower than OP elasticity of demand will be less than 1; and at price OP
elasticity of demand will be unity.

If we translate this into total revenue terms it will be seen that as the
monopolist sells output up to OX his total revenue will be increasing. We can see
that as more output is being sold up to OX, there is a gain in extra revenue (MR)
even if the MR is diminishing. But at output OX the total revenue must be at a

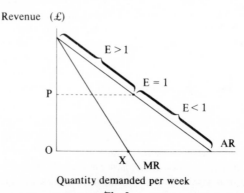

Fig. 5

maximum, because any further sales of output would mean that total revenue would fall as seen with MR becoming negative for the first time.

Thus increasing sales (or reducing price) up to OX will increase total revenue, but increasing sale (or reducing price) past OX will reduce total revenue. This means that reducing price down to OP will increase total revenue, but reducing price below OP will reduce total revenue.

We can say that a monopolist will never operate at a price level less than OP or an output level more than OX (i.e. where demand is inelastic) because by reducing output within this range he could increase his total revenue. Assuming that his MC was positive, he would not be maximising his profits within this range because MR would be negative here. Therefore a monopolist will always produce at a price where demand is elastic.

Referring to the essay title, we can now say that a monopolist could benefit himself by increasing his product's price within an inelastic demand range—because total revenue would be increasing and total costs falling—but no monopolist would operate within that range (if he is a profit maximiser) because MR would be negative in that area.

The monopolist will simply raise his price until he is selling an output where MR equals MC, and this will be in a price range where demand is elastic.

3. Which price will a monopolist charge?

A monopolist when faced with a given cost structure is able to charge a number of different prices (under different circumstances). This can be illustrated by marking these prices on Fig. 6.

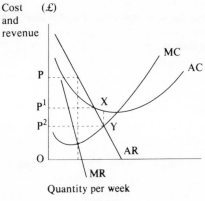

Fig. 6

a. Maximum profit price: this is where MR = MC, the price being OP.
b. Normal profit price: this is where AR = AC, the price being OP^1.
c. Marginal cost price: this is where AR = MC, the price being OP^2.

In case **c.** where the allocation of resources is supposed to be optimal, we can see that the monopolist (a nationalised industry?) would certainly need a subsidy (XY) to cover the loss being made.

Essay questions

1. *'Monopolies are undesirable, therefore mergers should not be allowed'.*
   Discuss.   (Lond.)
2. *Do monopolists necessarily act against the consumer's*
   interest?   (Oxf.)
3. *Discuss the view that monopoly is an evil. What types of economic*
   policy are used against monopoly?   (JMB)
4. *In what ways and to what extent can the sole producer of a product*
   control the level of profit he obtains?   (O/C Board)
5. *Explain why in certain circumstances the price charged by a monopolist*
   might be lower, and the output produced higher, than if an industry
   were perfectly competitive.   (WJEC)

Brief comments on essay questions

Question 2

The operative word in this question is 'necessarily', as it enables the answer to be divided into two main parts preceded by a short introduction.

Suggested Format:

1. Introduction:

   a. Definition (sole producer, no close substitute, barriers to entry).

   b. Diagram showing the equilibrium position of a monopolist.

2. Traditional case against the monopolist:

   a. higher price;
   b. lower output—less than optimum size;
   c. super normal profit even in long run;
   d. inefficiency and waste;
   e. lack of urgency in producing new ideas, techniques and progress;
   f. Ability to discriminate in prices.

   Critics of the monopolist would say that circumstances do not allow resources to be allocated efficiently. As average revenue is always greater than marginal revenue (and as maximisation of profits involve MR and MC being equal) then average revenue (or price) is bound to be above marginal cost. This condition of P > MC is the central feature of the inefficient allocation of resources in that consumers measure the valuation of a marginal unit of a good by its marginal cost. If consumers are paying a price in excess of marginal cost, they are indicating the value they place on the marginal unit is higher than it costs to produce. Therefore the welfare of consumers would be improved if production were expanded to the point where price and marginal cost were equal.

3. Arguments in favour of the monopolist:

   a. attainment of economies of scale and lower costs;

   b. nationalised industries involve a saving in fixed capital—lower prices are subsidised;

   c. possession of resources for research enables technical progress to be made.

Suggestions for further reading

Cairncross, A. K., *Introduction to Economics*. (Butterworth, 1973.) Chapter 17

Giles, C. ed., *Understanding Economics*. (Manchester Project—Ginn & Co., 1971.) Chapter 11

Harvey, J. *Modern Economics*. (Macmillan, 1974.) Chapters 13–14

Hewitt, G. *Economics of the Market*. (Fontana/Collins, 1976.) Chapters 8–9

Lipsey, R. G. *An Introduction to Positive Economics*. (Weidenfeld & Nicolson, 1975) Chapters 21–24

Stanlake, G. F. *Introductory Economics*. (Longman, 1971.) Chapters 15–16

Essay number 10

If a country's national income rose by 25% in 10 years, would its inhabitants necessarily be better off? Give reasons for your answer. *(IB)*

Suggested answer

The national income of a country is made up of the flow of goods and services produced by that country over a specific period of time. It is a flow of wealth and can be looked at in terms of output produced, income earned or expenditure released.

The national income is measured in money value terms and thus it has two main components—price and quantity—which when multiplied, will give the total money value of the output of a country.

Whichever method of calculation is used there are difficulties involved in reaching an accurate conclusion, and so complications such as double counting, transfer payments and indirect taxation/subsidies make it clear that national income figures are still estimates.

Perhaps the most important point to note in attempting to relate national income to economic welfare is the fact that the value of money changes over time. A rise in the money value of the national income may come about, but instead of it being the result of an increase in the volume of real goods and services, the prices of a known quantity of output may have risen instead. The standard of living of a community is determined by an increase in real output, not merely a money value. To answer the question we need to know the change in the price level over the same period to see whether there was a real physical change in output.

The inhabitants of a country are the producers of the national product, but even an increase in output in real terms would not make the average individual better off if the population had risen by a larger percentage. If the national income is divided by the population figure, we can obtain the national income per head, and this is a much more revealing statistic.

The rise in national income per head has still to be considered in conjunction with the distribution of this income, because such a rise in income might be associated with a redistribution of income in favour of the rich. The gain in their economic welfare may yet be outweighed by the loss in welfare of the poor.

While the physical volume of output might have expanded over the years, the type of product produced must be considered carefully. The production of goods and services for defence purposes may well be essential to protect the political well being of the nation, but one can scarcely say that a country's standard of living has increased. Scarce resources are being utilised in one way and therefore cannot be used in any other way. In the same way the production of producer goods may well lead to growth prospects in the future but current living standards are reduced.

Finally the 25% rise in national income may well have been the result of a longer working week and a greater effort on behalf of the workers. One might have found an increasing proportion of working mothers in industry to the detriment of family life. Before one can suggest that standards of living had risen, stock has to be taken of the community's own valuation of its leisure compared with its materialism. The seemingly endless quest for material welfare is being challenged by the cost society has to bear in the ever congested cities, the polluted atmosphere and the more complex life society has to endure.

Despite all these qualifications, it is still possible to use the national income per head as the best indicator of a country's standard of living, but it must be used with caution.

Comments

A. Specific points

1. Division of the essay into **two** sections:

   a. Definition of national income—a short introductory paragraph.

   b. Qualifications to the view that people will be better off—this should form the major part of the essay.

2. Points of Emphasis:

   a. Although measured in money terms, the national income is a collection of physical goods and intangible services. It must not be confused with the government or national revenue (which is the income of the government).

   b. Candidates must show the relationship between national income and economic welfare.

   c. The essay should include about half a dozen main limitations to the accepted view that an increase in national income should be equated with an enhanced economic welfare for a country's citizens.

   d. Interpretations differ, but the question does *not* call for an exhaustive account of the different methods of calculating the national income.

B. General points

1. Make sure you understand the following terms:

   a. imputed value   **e.** capital consumption
   b. value added   **f.** stock appreciation
   c. final goods   **g.** disposable income
   d. factor cost   **h.** double counting.

2. How is the national income affected by price changes?

Remember that the national income is a physical concept—a quantity of goods and services which is given a monetary value. Comparisons of national income totals over a period of time may give false impressions of increased living standards. But it is the *real* change in physical quantity which is important, a fact often disguised by the existences of price changes.

For example: if the national income of a country rose from £10 billion to £20 billion over a given period of time, it has shown a 100% increase. If prices remained constant during that time period, the change would be a 100% increase in real income. However, if prices rose within that period by 50% some candidates might feel they have to adjust that increase in income by one half, giving a real income increase of only 50%. This is a *false* calculation which many candidates employ. The procedure is to alter the figure of £20 billion so that it does not contain any price increase, and then compare this new figure with the original £10 billion, to give a correct percentage change. The calculation will then have been made at *constant* prices.

The appropriate method is one of utilising the technique of index numbers so that the £20 billion can be deflated to a realistic or non price-assisted figure. If the price index is given a value of 100 in year 1, a 50% rise in prices would give a price index of 150 in year 2.

Therefore £20 billion when expressed in terms of year 1 prices will be

$$\frac{£20 \text{ billion}}{1} \times \frac{100}{150} = £13.3 \text{ billion}$$

The national income has increased from £10 billion to £13.3 billion which is an increase of 33.3% (and not the 50% many candidates might be inclined to state).

3. Which are the common difficulties encountered when calculating national income?

There are **three** ways of identifying and measuring the national income:

a. by adding together all incomes earned by the different factors of production as they provide goods and services;

b. by adding together the value of everything produced;

c. by adding together the value of all the community's final expenditure. Each method is fraught with certain difficulties, and it would be wise to isolate three or four of the major ones.

Difficulty Number One:

Question: Which incomes should be included in national income estimates?
Answer: Only those incomes which have *contributed to the current production* of goods and services.

The expression 'one person's spending is another person's income' implies that every income is to some extent a transfer. This fact should not debar an income from being included in national income estimates. The crucial determinant is whether the income being considered has contributed to the current production of goods and services. If there are economic assets to put alongside the income, then that income must be included in any assessment. It is quite different for a person to 'acquire' an income in the form of social security payments, interest from national debt securities or even acceptance of subsidies. These really are 'transfer payments' which have come from government sources. It *does not matter where these incomes have come from*; what does matter is that the recipients have not contributed currently to the national wealth. In fact some government payments must be included, such as the incomes of policemen, members of parliament and the members of the armed Forces. They are all producing current services, and their incomes help increase the national product.

A further complication occurs in that if we should include everything the nation produces, some productive actions receive no payment making it extremely difficult to place a money value on the action. The invaluable services of the housewife, the ability of some husbands to undertake 'do it yourself' work, and the farming community's decision to consume part of their own productive efforts, are all examples of important services upon which accurate monetary values cannot be placed. Consequently they tend to be ignored in national income calculations.

Based on the following data, what amount of income would be included in the calculation of the national income? A schoolmaster, happily married, earns £5,000 p.a. He gives his wife a housekeeping allowance of £10 per week, and contributes to his son's university grant to the extent of £500 p.a. His wife works part time in a hospital earning £500 p.a., £250 of which she uses to employ some domestic help in the house. Your answer should be £5,750.

Difficulty Number Two:

Question: What is meant by the term 'national income'?
Answer: It it is the GNP minus depreciation.

Commentators may well use the term 'GNP' (gross national product) in economic forecasting, but it is not strictly true to equate this term with the other more commonly used term 'national income'. Confusion often arises over these seemingly similar terms, and the inclusion of 'gross domestic product' (GDP) does not make it easier.

Every country, within its boundaries, possesses a certain amount of resources which may well be owned either by the residents of that country or even foreigners. But whoever actually owns the resources, the overall output produced from those resources is called the GDP. The term 'domestic' refers to the output emerging from within a country irrespective of the actual ownership. In fact foreigners own resources in the UK and there are British owned assets abroad, both of which result in a two way movement of profits into and out of the UK. When the two flows are added together the total, usually positive, is called 'net property income'. When this figure is added to the GDP the resultant figure is known as the GNP.

There is still another adjustment to be made before arriving at the national income. Some part of a country's resources are used to maintain the capital stock from deteriorating, an amount known as 'depreciation'. It is only when this is deducted from the GNP that we can see the real volume of consumer goods and services, and net addition to the nation's stock of capital, which is available to the inhabitants of the country.

The following equations sum up the relationships:

GNP = GDP + net property income from abroad;

GNP − depreciation = national income (net national product).

Difficulty Number Three

Question: How are market price calculations adjusted to factor cost values?
Answer: By deducting indirect taxation values and adding subsidy values.

The expenditure method approach in calculating the national income suffers from the fact that the statistics used (from the Census of Distribution and Census of Production) produce values measured at market prices, i.e. the prices paid by purchasers. The final figure gives the impression that it stands for the cost of the resources which went into the production of goods and services involved. But this figure is *not the same* as the amount of income received by the factors of production in payment for their services. There are **two** main reasons:

a. The price paid by purchasers usually contains an indirect tax so that the total amount spent does not all end up in 'the sellers' pockets. One would have to deduct the value of indirect taxation revenue from the expenditure figures for a realistic total to emerge. After all, the government does not want to be responsible for a fall in the national income every time it decides to reduce indirect taxation! In that event, a country's standard of living would be going up while its national income went down.

b. The purchase price of some goods (farm products, nationalised industries) is not a true reflection of the cost of producing the items, because the existence of government subsidies enables some goods to be priced below their actual cost. It is essential to add the total value of government subsidies to the market price figures for correct assessment.

The following equation will clarify matters:

GNP measured at market prices—indirect taxation + subsidies = GNP measured at factor cost.

Difficulty Number Four

Question: What are final goods?
Answer: Goods produced by an economy after eliminating double counting.

The impression may be given that final goods are those goods which households finally consume, i.e. consumer goods. In fact, final goods can be consumer and investment goods dependent upon the assumption one makes as to the state of the economy.

a. Imagine an economy consisting of firms and households, each group selling goods or services to the other in return for income—which is then *all* spent on the goods or services offered by the other group. Everything is spent; there is no saving. The GNP of this economy can be calculated by any one of the three main methods, but if the output method were chosen, the value of the output of each firm added together would be greater than the value of the output consumed by the households, owing to the existence of double counting. Every input bought by firms from other firms to further their production, are known as 'intermediate' goods, but their cost must be deducted before a 'value added' figure for each firm can be arrived at. In this economy all final products are consumer goods and are sold to households.

b. Now imagine a more realistic economy where households and firms both save and invest. Consumer and investment goods make up the total output, and are both regarded as final goods, in that the consumer goods are sold to households, investment goods are sold from one firm to another, and some investment goods known as inventories are produced by firms but not sold at all.

FIRM ⟶ sell final goods ⟶ FIRM ⟶ sell final goods ⟶ HOUSEHOLD
            | |
      Investment good   consumer good
      (capital equipment)   (television set)

Essay questions

1. *Examine whether total satisfaction or economic welfare increases when national income rises.*   *(CA)*

2. *'National income = national output = national expenditure'. Explain and discuss this statement.*   *(Lond.)*

3. *In what ways are the national income accounts of a closed economy with no government sector modified by*

   i. *the introduction of a government sector and*
   ii. *the opening of the economy to international trade?*   *(O/C Board)*

4. *Explain what the concept of national income attempts to measure, and briefly indicate the methods by which it can be estimated in practice.*

   Discuss how each of the following items affects the measurement of the national income of the United Kingdom.

   a. *Prize money on premium bonds*
   b. *Notional rent of owner-occupied houses*
   c. *Sales of shares on the Stock Exchange*
   d. *The wages of members of the police force.*   *(WJEC)*

5. *Are the problems of measuring national income per head in a country like Nigeria likely to be the same as in the UK? What do differences in two such estimates mean?   (JMB)*

Brief comments on essay questions

Question 2

Candidates might adopt the following pattern:

1. *What does the equation mean?*
It is merely another way of suggesting that there are three main methods used to calculate the same thing, i.e. the output of goods and services produced by a country in a given time period.

2. *What exactly are the three methods?*
Explain each method *briefly* **a.** output **b.** income **c.** expenditure.

3. *Various difficulties arise in calculation*
It is most appropriate to show how certain difficulties can be associated with a particular method:
a. double counting is dealt with by adding the values of the final products or totalling the value added at each stage of production;
b. transfer payments are dealt with by only including an income in the calculation if it has contributed to the national income;
c. factor cost is dealt with by remembering to deduct taxes and add subsidies from/to the market price valuation.

4. *The significance of such statistics*
a. There is a strong relationship between these national income statistics and the standard of living, and candidates must explain the major problem of the effect of the value of money changing.
b. The government makes a comprehensive analysis of national income statistics in its efforts to control and plan the future of the economy.
c. The statistics form the basis of international comparisons of living standards, but in this area even more difficulties emerge.
d. The social costs of pollution, noise and congestion are not included in the national income accounts.

Suggestions for further reading

Cairncross, A. K. *Introduction to Economics*. (Butterworth, 1973.) Chapter 25
Giles, C., ed. *Understanding Economics*. (The Manchester Economics Project—Ginn & Co., 1971.) Chapter 15
Harvey, J. *Modern Economics*. (Macmillan, 1974.) Chapter 24
Lipsey, R. G. *An Introduction to Positive Economics*. (Weidenfeld & Nicolson, 1975.) Chapter 34
Stanlake, G. F. *Introductory Economics*. (Longman, 1971.) Chapter 17
Whitehead, G. *Economics Made Simple*. (W. H. Allen, 1974.) Chapter 26

Essay number 11

'Savings and Investment are always equal by definition. Savings is equal to Investment only at the equilibrium level of income'. Explain the apparent contradiction between these two statements. Give a simple numerical example to illustrate your answer. (WJEC)

Suggested answer

Incomes are generated by production and the economic system is said to be in equilibrium when all the incomes earned are returned to the income flow through spending. This simple model system is affected by the existence of two complicating factors—saving and investment. Saving is that part of income which is not consumed and therefore not passed on in the income flow. Investment is the process of capital formation plus addition to stocks and therefore is an addition to the income flow.

The main reason for the apparent paradox in the title is that both terms, savings and investment, are defined differently in each statement.

When Keynes stated that saving was always equal to investment he was referring to a particular period of time which had already elapsed. Perhaps it would have given greater clarity to have used the words actual or realised saving and actual or realised investment. In this way perhaps one would have appreciated that one was studying the same identity from different time scales.

The income obtained from the production of the national output is distributed to the various factors of production employed in that production and so national income and national output are always and necessarily equal. They are merely the same thing looked at in different ways. The output produced will be either for current use or will be added to the country's holding of real wealth (investment goods). The income earned will either be used for consumer purposes or saved. As aggregate output and income are equal, and consumption is identical in both places, the rest of the equation must also be equal.

When we talk of saving and investment being equal, we are referring to the observed behaviour of an economy; a study of what has actually happened or what has been realised. But the Keynesian analysis of income determination revolves around the intended nature of such variables as saving and investment. These plans to save and invest help to initiate changes in the income flow which culminate in different equilibrium levels being reached.

Decisions to save and invest are constantly being made by different groups of people, at different times and for different reasons. There is very little chance of these plans being equal to each other within the same time period. When any discrepancy between the plans to save and invest occurs a change in the level of income brings about a state of disequilibrium, and as income continues to change so do these plans get readjusted until a level of income is reached where planned saving and investment are once more equal to each other. It is only then that equilibrium has been attained where there is no tendency for the level of income and employment to alter. This process is facilitated by a multiplied change in income which operates both in an upward and downward direction.

A simple numerical example may clarify the above.

(£ *million*)

Planned income	Planned consumption	Planned saving	Planned investment	Unplanned investment	Realised investment (planned & unplanned)	Planned expenditure
400	370	30	50	−20	30	420
500	450	50	50	0	50	500
600	530	70	50	+20	70	580

The table gives a consumption function, from which saving plans can be obtained. Assuming that planned investment is autonomous and that all household plans are realised, an equilibrium level of income can be calculated.

When income is 500 the consumption schedule indicates that 450 will be consumed, leaving the remainder (50) to be saved. At this level of income autonomous planned investment is 50, thereby bringing total planned expenditure (consumption + investment) equal to the level of output (or income). With planned saving and investment being equal, the economy is in a state of equilibrium—there are no forces at work changing the level of output or income.

However at the higher level of income (600), planned saving exceeds planned investment resulting in planned expenditure falling below planned income. As the rate of production exceeds the rate of sales by 20 the level of stock will rise thereby resulting in a rise in unplanned investment. Any stock changes are regarded as changes in investment. At this stage realised investment made up of planned and unplanned investment, will still be equal to realised saving, but the discrepancy between the intentions of savers and investors will result in the level of income falling back until it reaches the equilibrium level of 500.

If income were 400 the consumption schedule would indicate that 370 would be consumed and 30 saved. With planned investment exceeding planned saving, planned expenditure would exceed planned income resulting in a fall in the value of stocks (inventories). This fall in stocks can be regarded as unplanned disinvestment, giving a realised investment figure of 50−20 = 30 (which is the same as realised saving).

Comments

A. Specific points

1. Division of the essay into **three** sections:
   a. Equality of saving and investment in a definitional sense.

   b. Equality of saving and investment in a planned sense.

   c. Mathematical example incorporating both aspects.

   The three sections should be given equal emphasis.

2. Points of Emphasis:

   a. Time element—observed behaviour i.e. after the event, shows savings and investment always being equal. Intended behaviour is more likely to indicate a discrepancy between saving and investment.

   b. The prefix before the terms saving and investment is most important i.e. realised, actual, ex-post versus planned, intended, ex-ante. In a sense it is wise not to use the terms saving and investment on their own; they should be coupled with the appropriate prefix.

   c. Realised saving is equal to realised investment at all times and at all levels of income, irrespective of whether the economy is in equilibrium. Planned saving and planned investment are only equal at one level of income—the equilibrium level—and so at that level both planned and realised saving and investment are equal.

   d. The existence of inventories being regarded as investment help to bring about the equality of realised saving and realised investment.

   e. The numerical example should help to clarify matters, and will only do so if it is straightforward and simple—which is what the question asks for.

B. General points

1. Make sure you understand the following terms:

   a. investment as seen by an economist
   b. consumption function (or schedule)
   c. circular flow of income
   d. equilibrium income level
   e. autonomous expenditure
   f. realised investment.

2. What are 'inventories'?

   Firms often use capital goods to help them produce other goods which may be either consumer goods or even more capital goods. So any good which is produced but is not used for immediate consumption can be labelled an investment good. As the rate of output and the rate of sales may be at odds with each other through un-expected fluctuations in both purchasing decisions and production changes, all firms require a surplus stock of inputs, such as raw materials, and a surplus stock of out-puts, such as consumer goods (washing machines). Smooth production runs and delivery dates can then be met in spite of the difficulties of unforseen scarcities. These inventories are an important part of a successful business.

The existence of surplus stock costs the firm money but it is felt that it is worth while protection in a competitive environment. The firm regards these stocks as part of its investment. While it is essential for all firms to hold a certain quantity of inven-tories there may be enforced changes in this total due to the rate of production exceeding the rate of sales. In this case consumer goods which are not selling will ac-cumulate as stocks, and from a definitional sense there has been an increase in un-planned investment. The opposite case of a fall in stocks would count as un-planned disinvestment.

Which of the following items can be classified as inventories?

a. raw materials **b.** semi-manufactured goods or **c.** unsold consumer goods. (answer: all of them).

3. Why are Saving and Investment always and necessarily equal?

This question is the bugbear of many candidates. The statement is only true in a definitional sense because one has taken a period of time which has just elapsed. The part of the national output which was not consumed (saved) must have, by necessity, been added to and become part of the nation's stock of capital (investment). What was actually saved—when defined as that part of income not consumed—must have been equal to what was actually invested. The manner in which both terms are defined must make them equal.

Keynes confused both laymen and academics by emphasising, on the one hand, the equality of these variables, and yet, following it up by explaining the con-sequences of a discrepancy between the variables. The first part of the exercise was looking at the concepts after they had taken place and the second part was analysed before they had taken place.

An analogy can be given with demand and supply analysis, in that demand curves are merely statements of intentions of consumers' purchases at certain prices. Similarly supply curves indicate the plans of suppliers' offers for sale at cer-tain prices. These intentions can only be fulfilled at an equilibrium level. If price is not at equilibrium the separate plans will not be achieved and changes will occur in the price until they are achieved.

The amounts actually bought and sold are realised or ex-post quantities and they are obviously equal to each other. In fact at equilibrium the realised quantities are equal to the planned quantities.

By accepting the term 'inventories' as investment, and appreciating that a dis-crepancy between planned saving and planned investment will result in some of those plans not being carried out, a change in inventories will take place which is unplanned. In other words, at the beginning of a time period, plans to save may exceed plans to invest so that at the end of the time period entrepreneurs will still have unsold output on their hands, i.e. unplanned investment. Thus the saving made in the period will be equal to the planned investment plus the unplanned investment, i.e. realised investment.

Essay questions

1. *Does investment always equal savings?* *(Lond.)*

2. *Why is it that macroeconomic equilibria must necessarily involve 'planned' saving and 'planned' investment?* *(O/C Board)*

3. *How are savings and investment made equal to each other in an economy which is almost always fully employed?* *(O/C Board)*

4. *'The Keynesian theory of employment rests wholly on the relations between Saving and Investment'. Discuss.* *(SU)*

Brief comments on essay questions

Question 3

Candidates must realise that this particular essay is open to a number of different interpretations. It is framed in such a way that many of the key features of Keynesian analysis could be justifiably included in the answer. However *one suggested format* is as follows:

Introduction:
1. Define saving and investment in terms of their being a leakage and an injection.
2. The planned nature of both terms involve their being unequal at any moment in time—a state of disequilibrium.
3. A level of equilibrium brought about by the level of income changing.

Comparison of two types of economy:
a. Underemployed economy—an increase in investment will increase the income flow via the multiplier effect, and idle resources will become utilised. Out of the higher income level more will be saved until plans to save will rise to equal the increased plans to invest which initiated the process.
b. Fully employed economy—an increase in investment plans can only be in a 'money' sense as resources are already being fully utilised. For 'real' investment to take place, more resources must be allocated to investment goods, and this can only be accomplished by a fall in the production of consumer goods thereby releasing resources which can be channelled into the investment goods. It is probably the government's task to see that there are sufficient resources available for investment plans to be fulfilled, and so voluntary or compulsory saving is encouraged.

The *main feature* to be brought out in this essay is that in a fully employed economy investment goods and consumer goods are competing for the same limited resources, and an increase in the production of one type of good is usually at the expense of the other—in the short run.

An appendix: Keynesian analysis simplified

In 1936 J. M. Keynes's great work *The General Theory of Employment, Interest and Money* was published, the main aims of which were to analyse the causes of general unemployment. It was a veritable Sahara of economics; algebraic equations and abstractions interspersed with sections of calculus, and was incomprehensible to a large part of its reading public. But it stood classical theory on its head and shocked contemporary economic thought. He took 403 pages and 24 chapters to complete this work and yet he only required 18 lines (the full content of the first chapter) to indicate clearly the kernel of his argument.

To fully appreciate Keynesian analysis, a full understanding of classical orthodoxy is essential. Yet to produce a list of the main classical views from such an assortment of economists as Smith, Ricardo, Mill and Marshall one must be in great danger of implying that there existed a solid unified body of orthodox opinion which spanned nearly two centuries.

What follows is an attempt (incomplete though it may be) to draw together some of the main strands of classical thought and compare them with the challenging viewpoints of Keynesian analysis.

1. Classical thought assumed that the normal state of affairs was one of an economy which was either fully employed or returning to a full employment position. Keynes felt that full employment was only one of a number of different situations in which an economy found itself, the more normal one being an economy less than fully employed. Why should an economy's spending power, the decisions of which lie in the hands of millions of people, always bring about the required level of expenditure to produce an output level requiring a fully employed labour force? Surely the private enterprise mechanism can't be relied upon to respond so accurately!

2. The French economist, Jean Baptiste Say (1767–1832) supplied the supposedly foolproof assumption that an economy was in a constant state of full employment. He is linked with the quotation 'supply creates its own demand', which means that as any output produced creates an income for the producers, then their spending power will be enhanced to such an extent that general overproduction of goods would be impossible—thus no general unemployment can exist. Occasional disturbances in this pattern were met by the health giving powers of *laissez-faire* which allowed the signalling process of the price mechanism to reallocate resources until supply and demand were again in equilibrium. Keynes accepted that all income generated *could* be spent on buying up the product, but disagreed with the assertion that all income *would* be spent. Income would not tend to automatically regenerate itself. As real income increased, so would consumption but by less than the income. The gap had to be filled, thereby maintaining the income level, and this task was the preserve of investment undertaken by entrepreneurs. He did not accept the magical qualities attributed to *laissez-faire*, and felt that insufficient private investment must be made good by positive government action. Government intervention, through deficit financing, was necessary to haul an economy out of the depths of a depression.

3. The classicists appreciated that some income would be saved thereby breaking the income flow. This was countered by their suggesting that it would automatically be invested. They had a case as the only people capable of saving in the nineteenth cen-

tury were landlords and merchants, who themselves did the investing. Saving was investment by another name. Gradually as saving and investment came to be carried out by different people, for different reasons, and at different times, there was bound to be a discrepancy between the amounts, but the classical economists put great faith in the flexibility of interest rates to bring saving and investment into equality. Keynes dispensed with the rate of interest as the main variable for bringing saving and investment back into line, and introduced the idea that it was the level of income which everything revolved around. An increase or decrease in saving or investment would affect the income flow, and this would rise or fall until an equality had been reached between saving and investment.

4. The classicists believed that while an economy was always fully utilised, it was possible to expand that capacity by increasing investment. But before such capital formation was able to take place saving was necessary to provide the available funds. They believed more than this in that a community had to initiate saving before investment was forthcoming. The savers of society were the saviours of society. The fate of future consumers was in the hands of present consumers; funds would only be made available if present consumers saw fit to save and this savings amount fixed the amount invested which expanded the capacity of the country. The future was to be decided by the current consumers' decision to save.

Keynes did not agree that saving was the prime motivator and determining factor in the system. In fact he saw it in reverse—it was investment decisions which held the key and they were determined by a whole host of factors culminating in the expectations of an uncertain future. The virtuous role of savings was removed by Keynes and given a more evil role. An increase in the intentions of people to save may cause a cut in spending power and a fall in income. Should this result in reduced investment, then total saving would in fact decrease. The productive capacity of an economy does not determine the level of employment within that economy, as intimated by the classicists. It is the level of spending power which is the determining factor and as investment tended to be an erratic variable this was the prime determinant of the level of income, which in itself resulted in a given volume of savings. Investment determined saving, not the reverse.

5. Taking full employment for granted, the classical economists considered that any unemployment which did exist, occurred because the wage rate was too high to accommodate it. Unemployment could easily be eliminated by wage earners accepting lower rewards. Lower wages would mean lower costs and prices, which would bring forth increased sales and therefore more production and employment. They maintained that the wage level determined the employment level.

Keynes agreed with the idea that there was a relationship between wages and employment, but he reversed the causal relationship suggested by the classicists. He maintained that demand determined the level of employment which itself helped to determine the marginal product or real wage. Any increase in employment and production would reduce the value of the marginal product because of the law of diminishing returns, and with it reduce the average wage. He objected to wage cuts which supposedly would encourage more employment, saying that any action in this direction would make the position worse by causing a cut in spending power, leading to even more unemployment.

Conclusion

In a nutshell, Keynes maintained that employment was determined by the total 'effective demand' which itself depended on the propensity of the community to consume and the particular rate of investment in the country. He certainly demolished the status of the rate of interest as the traditional equilibrating factor, and introduced the new concept of liquidity preference. The kernel of his theory was the replacement of the rate of interest by the level of income as the chief mechanism of bringing about a state of equilibrium in the economy. Investment was an important variable and the key in the system, and Keynes suggested that it needed stimulating. When an economy was fully employed, a certain rate of savings would be taking place, and it was therefore essential that it be absorbed by an identical rate of investment. If the private sector did not feel it appropriate to invest in sufficient quantities, then Keynes implied that the government should take it upon itself to 'persuade' private industrialists to do so. One such way would be for the banking system to supply the quantity of money to influence the rate

The Keynesian Jigsaw Puzzle

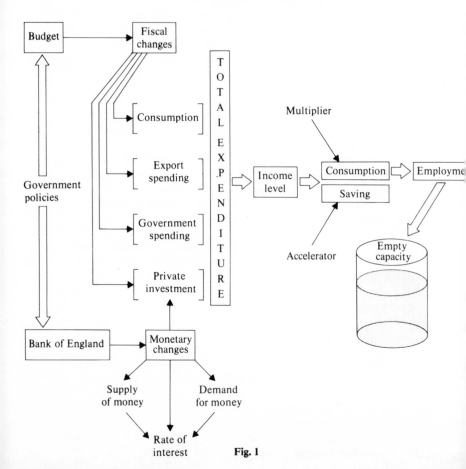

Fig. 1

of interest, so that investment might be affected. Other policies might be the government actually spending money themselves in the formation of public works, the aim of which would be not only to increase government investment, but to stimulate private investment by the use of the multiplier concept. Acting on the other main variable, the propensity to consume, it could also be stimulated by the government implementing fiscal policies so as to distribute incomes more equally.

Essay number 12

Why might an economy be in equilibrium at substantially less than full employment? Outline the measures open to a government to move the economy toward a full employment equilibrium. (O/C Board)

Suggested answer

The process of producing the national output generates a flow of income which is fed back into the system by purchasing the national output. A state of equilibrium emerges when all the incomes earned are in fact spent.

The real world economy is complicated by the existence of injections and leakages which affect this smooth income flow. Injections (government expenditure, investment and exports) are additions to the income flow, while leakages (taxation, saving and imports) are withdrawals from that income flow, and both will disturb the general level of this circular flow of income.

In Fig. 1 we can see that if an economy is at OB, there is insufficient spending power (DC) to buy up all the output. This will mean that the withdrawals are in excess of injections and firms will be receiving less than they are paying out in incomes. The economy will move back to a new lower level of income where equilibrium will be achieved at OE. At this point, planned withdrawals are equal to planned injections, or all income is spent.

Although it is always possible for an economy to generate sufficient income to buy up whatever its total output happens to be, the size of that total output is mainly dependent on how much money is actually spent. Every economy has a particular capacity to produce the national product, but an economy does not automatically produce a full employment level of output. The aggregate monetary demand within that economy may be at such a level that there are still idle resources remaining.

We can see that if firms plan to produce more than consumers plan to buy, stocks will accumulate and output plans will be adjusted downwards.

Expenditure (£)

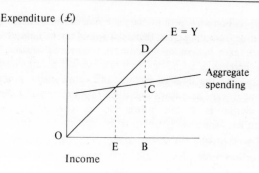

Fig. 1

Planned expenditure will finally be made equal to planned output at a lower level of income, but this level of spending will not encourage a full employment level of output to be achieved, and yet the economy is in equilibrium. If we assume that OB is a full employment level of output, then a deflationary gap or deficiency in demand of DC will arise, which will result in the economy finally settling in equilibrium at OE. This income level is not large enough to ensure a fully employed economy.

The economy, operating at an underemployed level, can be fully utilised if action could be taken on the main components of aggregate monetary demand. The government is able to make use of both monetary and fiscal policy with the intention of raising the consumption, private investment and export variables.

By lowering interest rates and increasing the money supply there could possibly be some favourable effect on consumption and private investment, and even a rise in the value of exports. But there is much scepticism as to the overall effectiveness of these policies. Hire-purchase restrictions can be eased so that consumer spending on certain consumer durables would expand.

Fiscal policy has been used in a demand management sense ever since Keynes's ideas began to take effect, and consumption, investment and government spending can all be raised. By reducing direct and indirect taxation, consumption spending can be increased. When taxation is reduced the disposable income of the economy rises and people will spend more on consumer goods. Private investment might be stimulated by tax cuts, particularly if corporation tax were reduced. Any initial change in this spending would have a multiplier effect on income based on the current marginal propensity to consume.

When the government increases its own expenditure, other things being equal, the effect on income will again be multiplied, and if this spending involves such items as social security payments or family allowances then the recipients are usually people with high propensities to consume, resulting in a rise in consumption.

Finally the government need not deliberately incur a budget deficit to achieve these aims of raising the expenditure lines. In fact even though a balanced budget is achieved there could well be a net increase in spending.

If £1 million was spent by the government and £1 million was taken in tax revenue from the public, the result would not be neutral as some of the income taken in taxation would have been saved initially. There would be a net increase in spending. This itself would be amplified by a multiplier effect, and the level of income and employment would expand. These changes can be shown by Fig. 2 where initially the economy is in equilibrium at OE but underemployed. Assuming OF is the full employment level spending power must be increased by AB for that income/output level to be maintained.

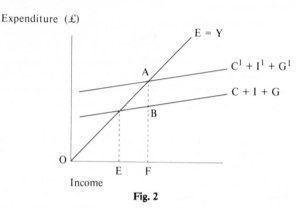

Fig. 2

By government action the C + I + G line can be raised to $C^1 + I^1 + G^1$. The economy is now in equilibrium with its resources fully employed.

Comments

A. Specific points

1. Division of the essay into *two* sections:

   a. Explanation of equilibrium and a full employment economy.

   b. Discussion of government policies to achieve full employment.

   Each section should be given equal prominence.

2. Points of Emphasis:

   a. Explain that the *circular flow of income* forms the basis of equilibrium study. While 'micro economics' assumes the level of income as given and concentrates on how resources are allocated based on a study of relative prices, 'macro economics' is concerned with the size and determinants of this flow of income and uses different models of the flow of income to help understand the effects of certain variables within these models.

b. *The model* used can range from very simple to extremely complex, giving different conditions for equilibrium dependent upon the model used, bearing in mind that they are all abstractions from the real world—which is inevitably more complex than the most advanced model.

c. A comparison of *equilibrium national income* and *full employment national income*. Before an equilibrium situation can be explained the assumptions for the model must be indicated first and the approach adopted could be either:

i. the income/expenditure method, or

ii. the savings/investment method.

The full employment level of income is simply that level of income which an economy is capable of producing when it is fully utilising all its resources. However, it must be made clear that an economy may be in equilibrium when resources are **i.** fully employed or **ii.** under employed. So the condition of equilibrium is *not* necessarily a bonus point for an economy.

d. *Government policies* are numerous and the question asks for an outline, not a complete examination of all the implications of the measures. Candidates must show they have a *full* comprehension of the armoury of government measures and on what variables they act.

Two items are called for:

i. main measures—monetary policies, fiscal policies;

ii. main recipients of those measures—Consumer spending; investment spending (private); export spending.

(Government investment is not included because it is the government taking the action although it is the public sector which is the receiver of the central government's decision making.)

B. General points

1. Make sure you understand the following terms and concepts:

a. macro economics	**e.** induced spending	**i.** balanced budget
b. aggregate demand	**f.** withdrawals	**j.** fiscal policy
c. investment	**g.** deflationary gap	**k.** propensity
d. autonomous	**h.** equilibrium	**l.** 45° line.

2. Why have assumptions when studying a model?

Keynes was interested in solving the unemployment problem of the 1920s and 1930s and concentrated his ideas on the 'short period' i.e. a period of time during which the capacity of an economy is fixed, and governed by the amount of existing resources. His thesis was based on the influence of total expenditure and its encouraging effect on employment. He saw real income rising as a result of spending by the community. Any models used require strict assumptions about the state of the economy in question, as the effect of the main variables can then be isolated. We can see demand, employment, income and output all responding in a *direct* relationship.

By assuming that the economy is underemployed and that the capacity is fixed, any expansion in demand will result in real output rising from the use of the previously idle resources. With prices also assumed constant, any change in employment and income of the community will reflect a real change in output (not merely a monetary change). Even an increase in investment spending is assumed to increase demand but not the growth prospects of the economy.

Once a clear understanding of the complex forces within the economy has been achieved, the assumptions can be dropped, and further analysis of the real world continue.

3. A closer look at 'Equilibrium income'.

Two approaches are usually implemented:
a. saving/investment method; **b.** income/expenditure method.

a. *Saving/Investment method*

The households and firms in the model make decisions, the interaction of which affect the level of income, bringing about new equilibrium levels.

Decision: Households distribute their income between money to be spent on consumption, and money to be saved. Saving is that part of income not spent on consumption and therefore not passed on in the income flow—it is an example of a withdrawal.

Decision: Firms decide to spend money on the purchase of *new* capital equipment. The decision has little to do with the plans of the savers, and is an active spending decision. It is an example of an injection because the income of a firm selling an investment good to other firms will have risen, even though household expenditure has remained constant. The flow of income has expanded.

Some main differences:
  i. 'Saving' means the same from the point of view of laymen or economists. But 'investment' by the layman is regarded as the purchase of securities; it is a money concept. The economist regards investment as a resource concept. There must be a net increase or additional real capital created; a replacement of idle resources into equipment, buildings or inventories.
  ii. Saving means the non-use of resources, while investment requires the use of resources.
  iii. Plans to save and consume are dependent on each other; they show an inverse relationship. Plans to save and investment are independent of each other.
  iv. The source of the funds for savings is the income level of the economy whereas the source of investment funds is not only savings (personal savings and undistributed profits) but also created money by the banking system.

v. Realised saving always equals realised investment but planned saving is only equal to planned investment at equilibrium.

The graph used (Fig. 3), indicating this approach, shows expenditure and saving on the vertical axis and national income on the horizontal axis. Empirical studies have indicated that there is a stable relationship between consumption and saving i.e. APS (average propensity to save) is constant. We assume that investment spending is autonomous.

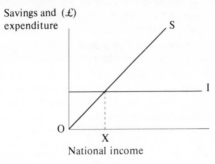

Fig. 3

It is essential to remember that all points on the graph indicate the *intentions* of households and firms to save or invest. At any income level other than OX the rival plans would differ, resulting in a change in the level of income of an expansionary or contractionary nature. Under the conditions given, there is only one equilibrium level, which is where the plans of the different parties are the same.

This approach needs qualification in order to cover the more complex models, as there are other withdrawals and injections to consider.

In an open economy with government, the full criterion for equilibrium would be:

savings + taxation + imports = investment + government expenditure + exports.
withdrawals = injections.

b. *Income/Expenditure method*
This is an aggregate approach concentrating on how much an economy is prepared to spend at different income levels. The current output generates an income, which, if all spent on that output, will help to maintain that level of output i.e. a position of equilibrium.

The graph used in this approach (Fig. 4) is usually known as the 45° diagram, showing expenditure on the vertical axis and national income on the horizontal axis. We assume that investment remains autonomous and that consumption is a constant fraction of income (i.e. APC is constant). By adding the values of the two linear curves, we arrive at the aggregate demand curve (E).

Some important points:

i. The 45° line is not a supply curve, but is a line joining all points where expenditure equals income (E = Y).

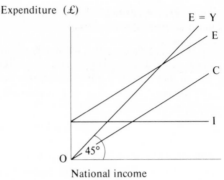

Expenditure (£)

National income

Fig. 4

ii. Saving plans can be calculated from the graph by the gap between the consumption line and the 45° line. Equilibrium can be seen by comparing the gap with the investment total, but this graph should not be used for that purpose. It is an aggregate expenditure graph.

iii. By drawing a consumption line so that it cut the 45° line it would indicate an APC which declined as income increased, and would give *dissaving* to the left of that intersection.

Again the statement that an economy is in equilibrium when planned aggregate expenditure is equal to national income must be conditioned by the fact that in an open economy there are two more injections to consider—government spending and exports. We can write the full equation as follows:

$$NI = C + I + G + (X–M)$$

(X standing for exports)
(M standing for imports).

4. Equations for Equilibrium:

Depending on the particular model of the economy being used, there are a preponderance of equations signifying the state of equilibrium. Most of them seem easily understood but there is one which causes problems with many candidates. It is the equation which terminated the previous paragraph. Comparing the two approaches, previously covered, the appropriate equations are as follows:

	Saving/Investment	Income/Expenditure
Simple economy	S = I (W = J)	E = Y (C + I = NI)
Governed economy	S + T = I + G (W = J)	E = Y (C + I + G = NI)
Open economy	S + T + M = I + G + X (W = J)	E = Y (C + I + G + (X–M) = NI).

E = aggregate expenditure   I = investment
Y = national income   G = government spending
C = consumer spending   T = taxation
S = savings   X = export spending
W = withdrawals   M = import spending
J = injections

The aggregate expenditure in an open economy includes **a.** consumer expenditure, **b.** all the injections (I + G + X). Why is it that to find the equilibrium level of an economy we have to deduct the value of import spending? Admittedly, import spending is still a withdrawal from the income flow but why not deduct all the other withdrawals as well?

The answer seems in fact quite clear in that some part of all the domestic spending contains an element of foreign purchasing, which must be deducted if we want to arrive at the national income figure.

Essay questions

1. *What is meant by the 'paradox of thrift' in times of unemployment? What measures can a government take to deal with this problem in times of recession?* *(CA)*

2. *Explain why, when national resources are not fully utilised, increased aggregate demand raises output. When national resources are used to capacity, what is the effect of increased demand?* *(IB)*

3. *Why is it thought necessary for the government to manage the economy? What are the main policy instruments available to the government?* *(O/C Board)*

4. *Explain the concept of 'an equilibrium level of income' and demonstrate why decisions to save must be matched by decisions to invest.* *(Camb.)*

Brief comments on essay questions

Question 3

The essay is clearly one of **two** parts, and adequate coverage should be given to both parts.

Part a.: Candidates might decide to concentrate all their available time on a full explanation of the deflationary and inflationary gaps. The use of diagrams in this case would be essential, and a developed answer could show that governments are aware of the problem of inflation and unemployment.

However a more comprehensive approach might be adopted with a survey of the whole range of government objectives being presented—not only the control of inflation and the reduction in the unemployment level but the attempt to achieve a balance of payments surplus and a steady growth rate. Obviously this latter approach would mean that a superficial coverage to the points would be expected.

Part b.: Candidates would do well to indicate that they appreciated all the government weapons capable of such control. The main Keynesian instruments used since the war have been fiscal and monetary policy, but regional policy along with exchange rate policy merit inclusion in the list. It would be incorrect to concentrate on one main policy such as a prices and incomes policy merely because a candidate had the detailed information of various phases to hand.

In this type of essay, candidates must be prepared to convince the examiner that they are fully conversant with *the overall picture*, and not merely knowledgeable on isolated aspects of the economy.

Essay number 13

Describe and discuss the main determinants in the level of investment. (Lond.)

Suggested answer

Investment can be defined as the expenditure on capital goods and addition to stocks, i.e. fixed-capital formation and inventories respectively. Newly produced capital goods may be used in two ways in that they can either replace existing capital assets which have depreciated, or be a real addition to the stock of capital assets held by an economy. It is the latter (net investment) which enables an economy to expand its capacity and grow.

The layman's interpretation of the term 'investment' implies the buying of stocks and shares on the Stock Exchange. This is merely a transference of securities already in existence and does not add directly to the nation's capital formation.

The volume of investment in an economy is not the sole preserve of the firms in the private sector, and the government is seen to play an increasingly dominant role in this. Central government departments, local authority enterprises and public corporations all make use of the scarce resources held by an economy in terms of capital investment. Roads, schools, houses and nationalised industries are expanded, and therefore may be using the scarce resources which could well have gone into the private sector.

The decisive factor determining investment decisions undertaken by private industrialists is the profitability or, rather, anticipated profitability of the project. The profitability can be said to depend on the expected future returns obtained from the purchase of the equipment, and the cost of borrowing the money to buy that equipment. The latter is specifically known before a decision is made, while the former can be thought of as nothing more than a calculated, if inspired guess.

The entrepreneur will know the cost of a particular machine and has to decide on the potential return from the equipment. To arrive at an answer, he must anticpate the life of the machine, the amount and cost of materials used in producing the output and the revenue returning to the industrialist which itself is dependent on the price and potential demand at that price. This entrepreneur may compare the known cost of the machine (the supply price) with the expected net return from the investment, but these future returns have to be discounted in order to arrive at a present value of expected earnings. This can be obtained by using the following formula:

$$\text{present value} = \frac{\text{expected revenue}}{1 + \text{rate of interest}}.$$

Keynes introduced an extremely complicated assessment of profitability into investment appraisal. He suggested that there was a particular rate of discount which could be used to discount expected future earnings until they were equal to the initial cost of a project. This marginal efficiency of capital (rate of discount) would be compared with the current market rate of interest to see if the project was economically viable.

Of course individual investments had different MECs and these could be aggregated into a downward sloping curve relating the amount of total investment projects to the differing marginal efficiencies of capital. In Fig. 1 OC represents the total of investments which have a marginal efficiency of 4% or more.

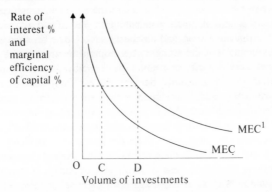

Fig. 1

If the rate of interest is placed on the same scale as marginal efficiency, then the current interest rate will help to determine how much investment will take place. If the current interest rate is 4% then all those investments with marginal efficiencies greater than 4% would take place. Any movement of the rate of interest will affect the volume of investment, but at the same time a change in the expected revenue coming from investment, will also raise the volume of investment to OD, as seen by a movement of the MEC curve to MEC[1].

A whole host of factors will affect an entrepreneur's estimates of the future earning capacity of his investment, including the current level of demand, the mood of optimism or pessimism as exemplified by current stock exchange prices and the prospect of further inflationary price changes. Particular attention must be paid to governmental policy changes, which through taxation changes and a system of grants, can either boost or deter investment hopes. Subsidies, investment allowances and tax rebates may well sway an industrialist in his decision making. Fundamental technical discoveries can lead to widespread purchasing of equipment, but may also lead to a revised assessment of the marginal efficiency of a project which might become obsolete.

The role of interest rates in investment determination is seen to be in grave doubt although it is realised that borrowing becomes more costly when interest rates rise. The size of the firm is important in that the larger companies may well be able to use part of their undistributed profits as a source of finance. Planning on a long-term basis which is common with large companies cannot be expected to be too easily influenced by short-term changes in interest rates. However governments can manipulate the rate of interest and this effect is shown through the money markets so that consumer demand at least might be affected. There is an undoubted relationship between a high level of demand and investment.

But it is not the absolute level of national income that determines investment. In fact, the crucial factor is the rate of change of the national income. When income is constant, investment will be limited to merely replacing equipment as it wears out. But as the rate of consumption increases it is necessary to increase the productive capacity to satisfy this new demand. A machine usually has a value far in advance of the value of its output in a year, and obviously has a longer life than consumer goods. Assuming that the economy has equipment which is fully employed, and that there is a certain amount of unemployed labour and resources, then an increase in consumer demand will eventually lead to an increase in investment (induced investment). We assume that any increase in consumer demand, say £1,000, will result in extra machines being produced, say £5,000. The new investment is said to be some multiple of the change in income. This multiple is called the accelerator coefficient, and it depends on the ratio of the value of capital equipment to the annual value of its output. Much will depend on the rate of change in income because if income rises at a constant rate, investment will be at a constant level. Any slow down in this rate of change in income may cause an absolute decline in the orders to the capital goods' industries.

Finally the government plays an important part within the total amount invested, with central government, local authorities and public corporations accounting for nearly 50% of the total. Here however the main determinant is not the profit motive, but political and social factors. Even cost/benefit analysis is used to evaluate the differing projects which a government might consider. We have seen governments using public works as a means to expand or restrain the economy, and the commitment to full employment has resulted on many occasions, in an expansion of investment in development areas.

Comments

A. Specific points

1. Division of the essay into **two** sections:

   a. Explanation of the term, 'investment'—a paragraph or two would suffice.

   b. An account of the main factors which influence investment—this would cover the major portion of the essay, but difficulties will appear when deciding on the emphasis to be given to the different determinants.

2. Points of emphasis:

   a. The layman's versus the economist's definition of investment—with the fundamental characteristic of increasing the productive capacity of an economy.

   b. The dominant role of the government in assisting private industry and its own public sector towards an expansion of investment projects. Gross investment stems from both the private and public sector, the motives of which differ.

   c. Empirical studies show that while consumption/or saving exhibits a constant and stable relationship with income, investment has proved an erratic and volatile variable, exhibiting tendencies of instability.

   d. The major part of the essay will be dominated by such terms as the rate of interest, marginal efficiency of capital, the accelerator, profit, etc. but candidates should try to communicate a wide understanding of the many determinants available, instead of concentrating on just one or two.

B. General points

1. Make sure you understand the following terms:

   a. depreciation
   b. productivity
   c. replacement investment
   d. rate of return
   e. historic versus replacement cost
   f. National Enterprise Board
   g. price code
   h. public investment

2. Which comes first—savings or investment?

   Pre-Keynesian economic thought accepted the fact that not only was there a direct relationship between the two variables, but the main determinant of investment was the expansion of savings. Post-Keynesian ideas accepted that there was a relationship between the two but that an increase in planned savings, other things being equal, would result in investment declining. This would occur in an under-employed economy with the level of income falling, and if induced investment is assumed, the level of total investment would fall until a new equilibrium point was reached. This 'paradox of thrift' meant that by attempting to save more, a community might make themselves worse off. The only occasion when an increase in planned savings was likely to lead to an increase in investment was when this economy was hindered by a lack of actual resources. Savings are necessary here to release resources from consumer use to allow their availability for investment purposes.

The correct interpretation of the interdependence of the two variables is that investment will determine the volume of savings by increasing the level of income, out of which a greater quantity of savings may be obtained—even though the propensity to save might not have altered.

3. What did Keynes mean by the 'marginal efficiency of capital'?

Assume that an entrepreneur is considering purchasing a machine costing £1,000 (the supply price), and that the current rate of interest he will have to pay to borrow the money is 5% p.a. The entrepreneur expects the machine to have a life of 4 years and the expected net earnings on using the machine will be as in the table, resulting in a total of £2,000 (the demand price). Should he compare the demand price with the supply price? Comparisons must be false if one is comparing a known with an unknown quantity. A pound note held now is more valuable than a pound note expected in the future as the present pound can be invested at a rate of interest. The method of finding the present value of some future earnings is by discounting the future earnings, utilising a particular formula, i.e.

$$\text{present value} = \frac{\text{expected revenue}}{1 + \text{rate of interest}}.$$

This procedure would be completed for *each year* and finally the total present value of that anticipated £2,000 will emerge:

$$\text{i.e. } \frac{600}{(1.05)} + \frac{550}{(1.05)^2} + \frac{400}{(1.05)^3} + \frac{450}{(1.05)^4} = £1,786.04$$

The entrepreneur can now make his decision by using this technique in one of two ways:

a. He could use the above approach using the current rate of interest (5%), and by comparing the supply price with the present value a decision can be made.

b. He could find a particular rate of discount which, when used to discount his future earnings (£2,000), would bring his present value equal to his supply price (£1,000). It must be extremely complex, if not impossible, for this rate of discount to be calculated, but entrepreneurs are assisted by the existence of statistical tables which make the job easier. This rate of discount can be called the marginal efficiency of capital and the entrepreneur will have to compare it with the current rate of interest (5%) to see if the project is commercially viable.

Keynes attempted to clarify matters by giving as his definition of MEC 'it is that rate of discount which makes the present value of the series of annual returns from the capital assets, over its life, exactly equal to its supply price'.

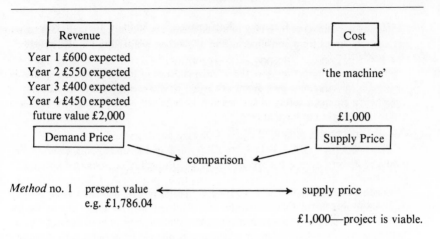

Revenue		Cost
Year 1 £600 expected		
Year 2 £550 expected		'the machine'
Year 3 £400 expected		
Year 4 £450 expected		
future value £2,000		£1,000
Demand Price	comparison	Supply Price

Method no. 1   present value ⟷ supply price
         e.g. £1,786.04

                       £1,000—project is viable.

Method no. 2   present value   made equal to   supply price
         e.g. if MEC is 8% which is greater than 5%—project is viable.

4. The significance of the Accelerator principle.

Investment may be divided into two categories—

a. *Autonomous investment*: i.e. investment which is not dependent upon current income. Examples of this would be 'replacement' investment which is the amount needed to compensate for the capital stock that passes out of service in that year.

b. *Induced investment*: i.e. any investment which takes place as a result of a change in demand.

What determines what? Is investment determined by or determining income? In fact it is both. This is yet another example of the circularity of economics. Which of the following statements is true? 'Investment is high when profits are high'. 'High investment results in a high level of income which causes profits'.

There is no argument over the connection between the demand for goods and services and the level of investment. But the acceleration principle required *certain assumptions* for the theory to be sustained:

a. capital equipment had a definite life of so many years, with a constant replacement demand for the equipment;

b. the equipment producing the consumer goods is fully employed and has no excess capacity—but there has to be some excess capacity within the capital goods industry otherwise the extra investment could not materialise;

c. firms try to maintain a constant capital: output ratio.

Taking an example to illustrate the acceleration principle: a particular industry is producing consumer goods with machines having an average life of 10 years, which necessitates a replacement demand of 10% of the capital stock.

Year	Sales	Capital stock	Replacement investment	Additional investment	Total investment
1	£1,000	£2,000	£200	—	£200
2	£1,200	£2,400	£200	£400	£600
3	£1,300	£2,600	£200	£200	£400
4	£1,300	£	£	£	£

Complete the blanks after reading the following paragraph!

When sales rise to £1,200, the extra £200 worth of consumer goods can only be produced if there is an extra production of £400 worth of equipment. During the year therefore £600 worth of investment has to be produced—£200 replacement, £400 additional. There has been a 20% rise in sales met by a 200% rise in investment, i.e. from £200 to £600 as seen in the Total Investment column. In year 3 sales rise by £100 requiring extra equipment of £200 to keep the capital: output ratio at 2. During this year £400 worth of investment had to be produced—i.e. a fall from £600 to £400 (£200 replacement, £200 additional).

Main conclusions

1. Any change in income (usually but not necessarily a change in consumption) produces a magnified change in investment, with the accelerator being the number which multiplies the increase in income to give the increase in investment.

2. A central feature is the 'rate of increase' and *not* the 'absolute level' of income.

3. *The elusive pimpernel: the <u>real</u> reason why investment is low.*

   Is it possible to offer a specific reason for the failure of investment levels in the UK? Here are a number of well-contested views all of which can claim support from certain sections of the electorate.

   a. Uncertainty as to the intensity and direction of government policy. Overall macro-economic management based on Keynesian philosophies and micro-economic interventions in specific areas of the economy have been responsible for the confusion set up in the minds of management. The inadequacy of government weapons has brought an instability to the economy which businessmen could not anticipate.

   b. Too high a level of corporate taxation destroys managerial enthusiasm and initiative.

   c. The inflationary bogey damages the management's desire to invest large sums. The apparently uncontrollable inflationary surge dampened investment decision making.

   d. Slumpflation, price controls and high interest rates collectively added to the difficulties of management in their efforts to combat the long-term downward trend in profits.

   e. Militant trade unions protected their security by restrictive practices, which led to the overmanning of equipment and the lowering of rates of return.

f. The incompetence of British management.

g. Low levels of wages have meant that the urge to modernise and replace labour by expensive capital equipment has not appeared.

h. Continual overseas investment has diverted scarce funds from investment starved British industry.

i. The City has failed to provide industry with the necessary funds.

Essay questions

1. *A certain machine costs £200 to purchase.*

   a. *If it has a life of one year and its output is expected to earn £220, is it a worthwhile investment if the rate of interest is 7% per annum?*

   b. *If the machine had a life of two years and would earn £121 in each year, would it be worthwhile if interest was at 10% per annum?*

   c. *What changes could lead to the opposite conclusion in either of these instances?* *(IB)*

2. *How might the government raise the level of private fixed investment in the UK?* *(Lond.)*

3. *What is the accelerator? To what extent can it explain changes in investment expenditures by firms?* *(Oxf.)*

Suggestions for further reading

Harvey, J. *Modern Economics.* (Macmillan, 1974.) Chapter 26
Lipsey, R. C. *An Introduction to Positive Economics.* (Weidenfeld & Nicolson, 1975.) Chapter 38
Livesey, F. *A Textbook of Economics.* (Polytech Publishers Ltd., 1978.) Chapter 6
Stanlake, G. F. *Macro-economics: An Introduction.* (Longman, 1975.) Chapter 6

Essay number 14

Discuss briefly what is meant by the multiplier, and consider why, in practice, a multiplier effect will involve the passage of time. What factors are likely to affect the value of the multiplier in an open economy with a government sector?   (WJEC)

Suggested answer

The concept of the multiplier was popularised by J. M. Keynes in the 1930s when ways to improve the employment position in the UK were being looked at. It rested on the fact that any increase in injections which occurred would not only increase total income but increase it by more than the initial injection of expenditure. The multiplier was the numerical value by which the injection had to be multiplied to equal the resulting increase in income.

The whole concept depended upon people spending part of any extra income they received but not spending all of it. As one person's spending was another person's income, the greater the proportion of extra income spent, the more would someone else receive. This process would continue with income increasing until the last penny was spent. The key factor in the multiplied increase in income was the marginal propensity to consume (MPC) or proportion of any increase in income which was consumed.

To illustrate this concept we have to assume that an economy which is underdeveloped, has an MPC of say four-fifths. Let us also assume that there is an autonomous increase in the level of spending which can come from one of the following categories—private investment, government spending, export spending or even the propensity to consume. To facilitate matters, a further assumption of a closed economy with no government sector can be added.

If an initial increase in investment occurred, income would automatically rise by that same amount to begin with, and this would be continued by the progression of the multiplier process. The recipients of the initial investment expenditure, say £10,000 would consume four-fifths of it, £8,000 and save one fifth, £2,000. Future recipients would spent four-fifths of any increase in their income e.g. four-fifths of £8,000 i.e. £6,400 and save the rest, i.e. £1,600. Further income would be generated until the initial £10,000 had been increased to £50,000 with the amount saved equalling the original investment amount. The economy has regained its equilibrium level, with people planning to save the same amount that firms are planning to invest.

The multiplier can be calculated from this example by realising that it is the ratio between an increase in income and the increase in autonomous spending which brought it about. But the determining factor is the MPC or from the saving side, the MPS. It is the proportion saved out of every increase in income which slows down the whole process of income growth. In the example, it is one fifth and so it becomes obvious that the multiplier will be the reciprocal of the marginal propensity to save, i.e.

$$\text{multiplier} = \frac{1}{\text{MPS}} \text{ or } \frac{1}{1-\text{MPC}}.$$

The above can be illustrated perfectly well in Fig. 1 where the autonomous increase in investment enables the economy to move from one equilibrium position OA to another one OB. The final increase in income AB is seen to be greater than the initial injection DC.

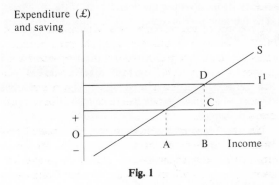

Expenditure (£) and saving

Fig. 1

In the real world, time-lags will be apparent in as much as consumers will require a certain period of time to adjust their spending habits to their increased income. Households may base their spending decisions in one time period on a previous period's income, and in the meantime any rise in income will lead to temporary unplanned savings while plans to consume are being revised.

Even producers cannot immediately increase output to satisfy increases in demand and stocks may be allowed to run down. Producers will have to be convinced that the increase in sales is permanent before they are willing to accelerate production.

In a closed economy with no government sector, the multiplier is dependent on the marginal propensity to save (MPS) only. There is only one withdrawal in this situation, savings, and so the larger the MPS the smaller will be the multiplier, i.e.

$$\text{multiplier} = \frac{1}{\text{MPS}}.$$

When a government sector is introduced, the existence of taxation may be regarded as a leakage and its inclusion will add to the size of the withdrawals thereby lowering the value of the multiplier, i.e.

$$\text{multiplier} = \frac{1}{\text{MPS} + \text{MPT}} \text{ (marginal propensity to tax)}.$$

With direct taxation being progressive, we find the rate of tax leakage increasing as income increases. The multiplier becomes smaller as the level of income rises. Furthermore if a tax change falls mainly on the less prosperous element in society, the effect on spending will be even greater than if the richer elements had to bear the main burden, because the MPC of the former is usually higher than the MPC of the latter.

An economy involved in foreign trade has to consider that proportion of its spending dealing with imports. This does help to meet a domestic demand but does not generate income at home. This type of spending is a withdrawal from the home economy's income flow and enters a foreign economy's income flow. The inclusion of this marginal propensity to import (MPM) must reduce the overall size of the multiplier.

The full multiplier is equal to the reciprocal of the marginal propensity to withdraw:

$$\text{multiplier} = \frac{1}{\text{MPS} + \text{MPT} + \text{MPM}}.$$

Comments

A. Specific points

1. Division of the essay into **three** sections.

   a. Definition and explanation of the multiplier.

   b. The significance of time-lags in consumption and production, and the connection with stocks.

   c. Show how the multiplier becomes smaller when government and trade influencing factors are considered.

   Parts **a.** and **c.** will account for the major part of the essay.

2. Points of emphasis:

   a. The central feature of the multiplier concept is the *marginal* propensity to consume and *not* the *average* propensity to consume.

   b. A numerical example (and/or diagram) is necessary to indicate the effect of an autonomous change in expenditure on the level of income.

c. The initiating factor will result in an induced change in both consumption and saving with equilibrium emerging only when the amount saved has risen sufficiently to be equal to the change in investment.

d. The existence of time-lags in spending and output decisions will not alter the appearance of the multiplier effect, but only delay it.

e. The existence of taxation and imports in the real world will add to the saving withdrawal and further reduce the value of the multiplier.

B. General points

1. Make sure you understand the following terms:

a. MPC/MPS
b. autonomous expenditure
c. paradox of thrift

d. output lag
e. induced consumption
f. reverse multiplier.

2. Some common sources of confusion:

a. Many candidates believe that the multiplier effect can only be sparked off by an expenditure change involving *investment*.

In fact the multiplied increase in income may be initiated by:

i. a rise in private investment;
ii. a rise in government expenditure;
iii. a rise in export spending; and even,
iv. an autonomous rise in consumption spending.

This last point means that the entire propensity to consume may have risen because of a change in spending habits or a fall in taxation. The consumption expenditure curve would have risen throughout its entire length.

b. Other candidates believe that the *numerical value of the multiplier* is affected by the injections taking place. Whether they take place or not, the existence of *a multiplier* remains within the economy. There is an extremely important distinction between **i.** 'a multiplied increase in income' and **ii.** 'an increase in the multiplier'—make sure you understand this distinction!

i. *A multiplied increase in income* can stem from (1) a rise in one of the injections assuming a given multiplier, as seen in Fig. 2; and (2) a rise in the multiplier assuming a given rate of injection as seen in Fig. 3. A change in the savings function from S to S^1 denotes a fall in the marginal propensity to save (or a rise in the multiplier)—see overleaf.

ii. *An increase in the multiplier* can stem from (1) a fall in the *marginal* propensity to withdraw—whether it be savings, taxation of imports—and (2) a change in the level of income brought about by a change in the injections.

This last point demands close analysis because it has been assumed up to now that the consumption function is linear (a straight line). In that case, the MPC is constant at its particular numerical value. However if the consump-

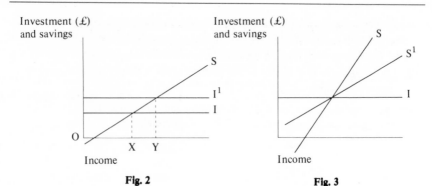

Fig. 2   **Fig. 3**

tion function is non-linear (a curve) then the MPC will fall as income rises during the multiplier process. Under these circumstances, any increase in investment which produces an increase in income will find the increases in income being multiplied by a different coefficient at each stage. The value of the multiplier would prove difficult to calculate, unless very small increases in aggregate income were considered.

c. Another complication for an accurate measurement of the multiplier is that *income is not necessarily spread evenly* throughout the economy. The average MPC of the inhabitants of the country will be affected by this redistribution of income. If the less prosperous element of the economy obtains the major part of the increased income, the multiplier effect will be much greater as the average MPC of this group of people is quite high.

d. It must not be imagined that the answer to an economy's ills is a simple injection of government expenditure or private investment leading to an expansion in output, income and employment. Much depends on the *state of the economy*: **i.** in an underemployed economy, an injection with a multiplier effect will lead to an increase in *real* income, **ii.** in a fully employed economy an injection with a multiplier effect will lead to an increase in *money* income, but not *real* income. The initial effect will be seen on rising prices, but real output will not rise unless the economy is able to release enough resources via saving so that real investment can take place.

e. It is usual to assume that any injections are autonomous, but in the real world *induced investment* will pose further complications. Any multiplied increase in income will lead to a rise in consumption. This change in the rate of consumption will induce a further expansion in investment and a further multiplier process will result. In other words, the economy will experience an accelerator effect, and may spiral into boom conditions.

3. The dynamic duo: APC and MPC.

A consumption schedule can be translated into graphical terms (Figs. 4–6) by plotting the relationship between consumption and income. Of the many consumption curves, whether individual or aggregate, there are three distinct types. From these curves, one can calculate the APC and MPC and study their relationships.

Fig. 4 *Curve number one*: a straight line passing through the origin.
Fig. 5 *Curve number two*: a straight line passing across the 45° line.
Fig. 6 *Curve number three*: a curved line (non-linear) cutting the 45° line.

Expenditure (£)

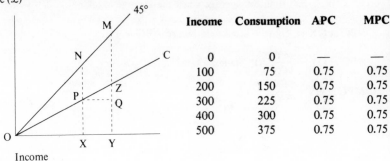

Income	Consumption	APC	MPC
0	0	—	—
100	75	0.75	0.75
200	150	0.75	0.75
300	225	0.75	0.75
400	300	0.75	0.75
500	375	0.75	0.75

Fig. 4

In Fig. 4 (1) Consumption is a constant proportion of income
(2) APC is constant at $\frac{3}{4}$ or 0.75 or 75%
(3) MPC is constant at $\frac{3}{4}$ or 0.75 or 75%
(4) APC = MPC

The basic difference between the calculation of APC and MPC is that APC is measured at a *given* level of income, but MPC requires a *change* in the level of income for a calculation to be made.

$$\text{APC at OX} = \frac{PX}{OX}$$
$$\text{MPC at OY} = \frac{ZQ}{XY}$$

Expenditure (£)

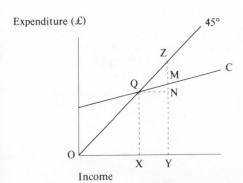

Income	Consumption	APC	MPC
0	50	—	—
100	100	1	0.50
200	150	0.75	0.50
300	200	0.66	0.50
400	250	0.62	0.50
500	300	0.60	0.50

Fig. 5

In Fig. 5 (1) Consumption is *not* a constant proportion of income.
         (2) APC declines with the level of income.
         (3) MPC is constant at $\frac{1}{2}$ or 0.50 or 50%
         (4) MPC differs from APC and is less than APC (the marginal must be
            less than the average when the average is falling).

APC at OX $= \dfrac{QX}{OX}$ (the breakeven point); APC = 1

APC at OY $= \dfrac{MY}{OY}$; APC is less than 1

MPC at OY $= \dfrac{MN}{XY}$

Expenditure (£)

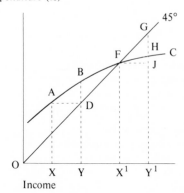

Income	Consumption	APC	MPC
0	100	—	—
100	160	1.6	0.60
200	200	1	0.40
300	220	0.73	0.20
400	235	0.58	0.15
500	245	0.49	0.10

Fig. 6

In Fig. 6 (1) Consumption is *not* a constant proportion of income.
         (2) APC declines with the level of income.
         (3) MPC declines with the level of income.
         (4) MPC differs from APC and is less than APC.

APC at OX $\ = \dfrac{AX}{OX}$ (this is greater than unity)

APC at OX¹ $= \dfrac{FX^1}{OX^1}$ (this is unity)

Thus APC declines with income.

MPC at OY $\ = \dfrac{BD}{XY}$

MPC at OY¹ $= \dfrac{HJ}{FJ}$

XY and X¹Y¹ are assumed to be equal increases in income.

BD is greater than HJ. Therefore MPC declines with the level of income.

Key Points on the relationship between APC and MPC

i. All straight line (linear) consumption curves going into the origin at whatever angle will have:
 a. constant APC (although a different constant APC for each slope);
 b. constant MPC which is the same as the APC.

ii. All straight line (linear) consumption curves cutting the 45° line will have:
 a. declining APC with income;
 b. constant MPC.

 Thus all straight line consumption curves will have a constant MPC.

iii. All curved (non-linear) consumption lines cutting the 45° line will have:
 a. declining APC with income.
 b. declining MPC with income.
 c. MPC being less than APC.

4. *The path towards the Real Multiplier.*

$$\text{The complete multiplier} \quad \frac{1}{\text{marginal rate of withdrawals}}$$

Marginal rate of withdrawals consists of: (a) marginal propensity to save;
(b) marginal propensity to tax;
(c) marginal propensity to import.

The following assumptions are made: national income = 10
consumption = $\frac{1}{2}$ of disposable income;
APC = MPC is constant;
marginal rate of tax is constant = $\frac{3}{5}$ of NI;
marginal propensity to import is constant = $\frac{1}{2}$
of consumption.

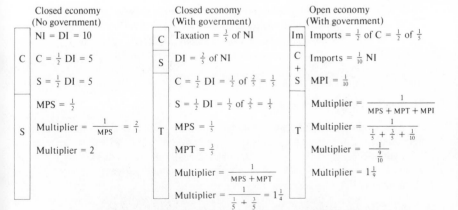

Closed economy (No government)

C | NI = DI = 10
| C = $\frac{1}{2}$ DI = 5
| S = $\frac{1}{2}$ DI = 5
| MPS = $\frac{1}{2}$
S | Multiplier = $\frac{1}{\text{MPS}}$ = $\frac{2}{1}$
| Multiplier = 2

Closed economy (With government)

C | Taxation = $\frac{3}{5}$ of NI
S | DI = $\frac{2}{5}$ of NI
| C = $\frac{1}{2}$ DI = $\frac{1}{2}$ of $\frac{2}{5}$ = $\frac{1}{5}$
| S = $\frac{1}{2}$ DI = $\frac{1}{2}$ of $\frac{2}{5}$ = $\frac{1}{5}$
T | MPS = $\frac{1}{5}$
| MPT = $\frac{3}{5}$
| Multiplier = $\frac{1}{\text{MPS + MPT}}$
| Multiplier = $\frac{1}{\frac{1}{5} + \frac{3}{5}}$ = $1\frac{1}{4}$

Open economy (With government)

Im | Imports = $\frac{1}{2}$ of C = $\frac{1}{2}$ of $\frac{1}{5}$
C + S | Imports = $\frac{1}{10}$ NI
| MPI = $\frac{1}{10}$
| Multiplier = $\frac{1}{\text{MPS + MPT + MPI}}$
T | Multiplier = $\frac{1}{\frac{1}{5} + \frac{3}{5} + \frac{1}{10}}$
| Multiplier = $\frac{1}{\frac{9}{10}}$
| Multiplier = $1\frac{1}{9}$

Fig. 7

Essay questions

1. *Examine how the interaction of the multiplier and accelerator may cause trade cycles or fluctuations in the national income.* *(CA)*

2. *Define 'the multiplier'. Discuss the effect of an increase in investment in conditions of (a) full employment, (b) unemployment.* *(Lond.)*

3. *What is meant by the marginal propensity to consume? Analyse the effect of an increase in the marginal propensity to consume on a country's output and on its price level.* *(Oxf.)*

4. *The following data represent net national product and consumption in an hypothetical economy.*

NNP	Consumption
100	100
120	116
140	132
150	140
160	148
180	164
200	180

   a. *Define and measure the marginal propensity to consume. Give the values of consumption when NNP is 80 and 220 and state the assumptions underlying your answers.*

   b. *Show how savings are related to consumption in this economy; give the value of the marginal propensity to save and explain what it means.*

   c. *Assuming that annual investment is constant at 10, what is the equilibrium level of NNP? Show clearly how you arrive at your answer.*

   d. *Show how the investment multiplier is related to the marginal propensity to consume in this economy. Give the value of the multiplier and explain what it means.* *(JMB)*

Brief comments on essay questions

Question 2

This essay calls for a *brief* definition and explanatory points regarding the concept of the multiplier. Candidates must avoid the temptation of being drawn into an over elaborate account of the multiplier, and must concentrate on a concise but accurate statement, so as to leave sufficient time to develop a comprehensive account of its significance in differing economies.

The major part of this essay must be subdivided as suggested in the title. With the aid of a diagram or diagrams, a clear analysis of how increased investment can affect an economy must be presented.

The basic difference between **a.** and **b.** is that inflation is likely to result in **a.** but an increase in real output will result in **b.**

As in most Keynesian essays of this type it is most helpful to direct a candidate's thinking process if a model is introduced with the related assumptions. An examiner can then see quite clearly that an answer is developing upon the right lines.

Suggestions for further reading

Harvey, J. *Modern Economics*. (Macmillan, 1974.) Chapter 26

Lipsey, R. G. *An Introduction to Positive Economics*. (Weidenfeld & Nicolson, 1975.) Chapter 36

Livesey, F. *A Textbook of Economics*. (Polytech Publishers Ltd, 1978.) Chapter 8

Marshall, B. V. *Comprehensive Economics: Part Two*. (Longman, 1974.) Chapter 12

Stanlake, G. F. *Macro-Economics: An Introduction*. (Longman, 1974.) Chapters 7–8

Whitehead, G. *Economics Made Simple* (W. H. Allen, 1974.) Chapter 28

Essay number 15

What factors are likely to affect the community's demand for money?
Consider the consequences of an increase in the demand for money if the
money supply remains unchanged.   (WJEC)

Suggested answer

Specialisation within economies can only function because of the existence of money. People want money because it is generally acceptable in settling debts, but the demand for money here is really a demand for commodities bought with money. The Keynesian interpretation of the demand for money is the idea of demanding a liquid asset. People require money because it confers on them the advantage of complete liquidity, i.e. it is readily convertible into any asset without incurring any cost. However, this has to be balanced against the fact that a liquid asset cannot earn any income, thereby sacrificing the interest one would gain from lending it. There is thus a demand for liquidity or a desire to hold one's wealth in a monetary form as opposed to a number of other alternatives, such as deposit accounts, shares or even real goods.

Keynes suggested that there were three main reasons why the community would want to hold more money. The transactions and precautionary motives were mainly determined by the level of income within an economy. Cash balances are required to finance day-to-day expenditures and these balances are even more necessary when the income level is rising, the inflationary rate is increasing or the frequency of being paid decreases. Extra cash balances are held as a protection against unforseen circumstances, and the more pessimistic a community, the greater the demand to hold money.

Active balances, as these two motives are known, are likely to be fairly stable and are not influenced by changes in the rate of interest.

Keynes emphasised that people held money over and above that required to meet the two previous motives. This speculative motive or idle balances is dependent on a person's expectation of changing market values in non-money assets. An alternative to money, which earns an income and can easily be disposed of, might be fixed interest government securities, so that the choice of holding money or stock would be dependent on the belief that the prices of that stock is going to change. If people believe that security prices are going to fall then there would be a desire on their part to be holding money and not stock.

The speculative motive depends on expectations of changes in the market price of fixed interest securities, but as there is a close inverse connection between market price and the current yield on this stock it is permissible to state that the speculative demand for money depends upon the expected changes in the current rate of interest (current yield). We can say that at low interest rates (high security prices) people will not find it such a great advantage to be in an illiquid state and earning an income. A community's liquidity preference at this stage will be high with people preferring to hold money balances. The foregoing can be illustrated by Fig. 1 where L^1 represents the active balances' demand, and L^2 represents the idle balances' demand.

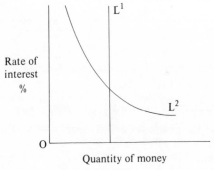

Fig. 1

An addition of these two curves will result in a curve representing total liquidity preference, sloping downwards to the right.

The concept of liquidity preference lies at the heart of the Keynesian determination of the rate of interest. The supply of money, indicated by the vertical line MM in Fig. 2, is determined by the authorities and is assumed to be fixed in the short run. When the liquidity preference curve, indicated by the curve LP, intersects the line, the result will be the current rate of interest OR.

When a community's liquidity preference increases, this will be indicated by an entire shift to the right of the curve as indicated by a new curve LP^1. The rate of interest is seen to rise from OR to OR^1. In fact this comes about by people wanting to increase their money balances in being prepared to sell securities. The sale of securities forces their price downwards resulting in their yield rising (the current interest rate rises).

This Keynesian analysis of the rate of interest has further connections with Keynesian employment theory in that an increase in the demand for

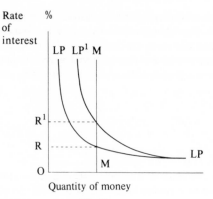

Fig. 2

money, other things being equal, will raise the rate of interest, which has a relationship with the Keynesian marginal efficiency of capital concept in that for any given interest rate there will be a determined rate of planned investment. The level of investment will be reduced and this will eventually lead to a fall in the level of income until a state of equilibrium is reached.

Comments

A. Specific points

1. Division of the essay into **two** sections

   a. The main determinants of the demand for money—two thirds of the essay.

   b. The effects of an increase in demand for money—one third of the essay.

2. Points of emphasis

   a. Distinguish between the *pre-Keynesian* view that the demand for money was in its use as a medium of exchange, and the *post-Keynesian* view that it was demanded as a liquid asset in its own right, so that money balances were demanded over and above the balances held to finance transactions. Thus there were (i) active balances and (ii) idle or passive balances.

   b. Money is one of a number of financial assets which are claims to the ownership of real assets, but not all financial assets (deeds of a house, shares, gilt-edged stock, bills of exchange) are equally acceptable in the settlement of debts. Only money possesses the quality of *liquidity*. The remainder can be termed 'near money' (anything which has to be turned into 'money' before it can be spent—money can be spent immediately in its existing form).

   c. A perfectly liquid asset has the advantage of 'liquidity' but the disadvantage of not being able to earn an income. Why do people demand to hold this type of asset—why have they got a *liquidity preference*? Keynes suggested three main reasons—transactions, precautionary and speculative motives.

   d. The *transactions* and *precautionary* motives are determined by the level of income mainly, while the *speculative* motive is determined by the expected future price of bonds (or the *expected* yield on those bonds).

It is important to remember that the key factor in the speculative motive is not so much the actual level of interest rates (or the level of bond prices) but the *comparison* between the present and the expected future rates.

e. By using diagrammatic form, the liquidity preference curve must be shifted to the right, taking into account the many assumptions for an accurate analysis, such as the money supply remaining fixed, and the Keynesian interpretation of the attitudes of people when faced by an inadequate supply of money holdings, i.e. they will sell bonds rather than cut down their expenditure on goods.

f. While the initial result of a state of disequilibrium in the demand and supply of money would be a change in the interest rates, it is worth investigating whether the changed interest rate might affect other variables such as investment and consumption, and perhaps the price level. This section would probably entail bonus marks in such an essay and involves a clear awareness of the main distinction between the role of money in a quantity theory environment and in a Keynesian environment.

B. General points

1. Make sure that you understand the following concepts:

a. speculative motive	**e.** current market rate of interest
b. liquidity	**f.** near money
c. bonds	**g.** liquidity trap
d. yield	**h.** velocity of circulation.

2. Common mistakes:

a. What is meant by 'the current rate of interest'?
There is no such thing as *the* 'rate of interest', as there are as many rates of interest as there are types of borrowing. In fact there is a *whole structure of interest rates* stretching from short-term to long-term and high-risk to low-risk loans. Within this structure there may well be relative movements in individual rates, but at times the entire complex will alter its position as it is influenced by changes in the demand for and supply of money. Financial commentators tend to refer to a single rate of interest as an indicator of this whole structure. We can simplify this even more as the array of short-term and long-term rates are represented by the Treasury bill rate and the yield on consols respectively.

i. *Treasury Bill Rate*: it is the average rate at which the discount houses will discount Treasury bills sold by the Bank of England. This rate is influenced by the extent of government borrowing through the sale of Treasury bills, and the minimum lending rate is correspondingly altered so that it becomes $\frac{1}{2}$% above the Treasury bill rate. At times, however, this automatic formula has been suspended, and the Bank of England takes it on itself to initiate the adjustment of the minimum lending rate.

ii. *Yield on Consolidated Stock* (irredeemable stock): Different types of government stock are issued with different fixed rates of interest attached and in units of
£100 nominal or par value. The fixed rate on government consols is $2\frac{1}{2}\%$ and it is
expressed as a percentage of the face value of the security. It is *not* the long-term
rate of interest, but these nominal fixed interest rates do reflect the level of long
term interest rates which prevailed at the time the government first issued the
stock. Today their market price will be significantly different from their nominal
price. The term 'yield' is the annual money income expressed as a percentage of
the market price of the stock, and is indicated by the following formula:

$$\text{yield} = \frac{\text{nominal rate of interest}}{\text{market price of stock}} \times \frac{\text{nominal value of stock}}{1}$$

The holder of $2\frac{1}{2}\%$ Consols will be guaranteed £2.50 per annum but as the
market price of the Consols might be £50, a new purchaser would find that
the purchase would provide a yield of 5%. It is this yield which is synonomous with the term 'current market rate of interest' and it is dependent
upon the changing market price of securities which will vary according to
buying and selling conditions.

Any new government stock about to be issued will have to pay attention to
the particular level of this yield, as new fixed interest rates will be based upon
it.

b. What is the *relationship between the rate of interest and the market price of
stock*?
This can be illustrated by the following example:

   i. A government stock, irredeemable, was issued at its nominal value of £100,
offering a fixed rate of interest of 2% p.a. Anyone buying this stock would
obtain a yield of 2%.

   ii. Five years later the general level of long-term rates rose to 10% p.a. so that
anyone buying government stock would obtain a yield of 10% p.a. At this
time if anyone bought the 2% government stock at its price of £100, that person would be forsaking an extra yield of 8%. The result was a fall in the price
of that stock until it reached £20, so that purchasers would then be obtaining
a yield of 10% p.a.

   iii. If a person holding this government stock expects interest rates to rise over
the year to 20% (or expects the price of stock to fall), it would mean that the
government stock he was holding would be priced in the market at £10.

   iv. He is faced with a choice of continuing to hold the stock or selling it. To hold
the stock the person would (a) gain over the year £2. (i.e. the fixed rate of interest), would (b) lose in capital loss the difference between the market prices,
i.e. £20 − £10 = £10. This would give an overall loss of £8.

The person would sell the stock and hold idle cash, i.e. increase liquidity
preference.

c. *Current interest rates* versus *expected interest rates*.
The rate of interest is the stimulus which persuades people whether or not to hold
their wealth in a particular form. The higher it is, the more one would tend to

hold an income earning asset, and the greater the opportunity cost of holding money. The liquidity preference curve simply relates the rate of interest (yield) to the demand to hold money.

Great emphasis should be placed on the role of expectations as the action taken by people merely serves to bring their expectations closer to reality. For instance, people do have an idea of what is the 'normal' rate of interest for a particular time period. If the rate of interest were to be in excess of this 'normal' rate, people would regard a fall in the interest rate as imminent. Looked at from the angle of stock prices, people would regard a rise in the price of stock as a strong probability. On this basis people will want to be in bonds rather than cash, and the purchase of bonds will take place. As the price of bonds rises the yield on them falls. Thus a higher interest rate than normal would encourage a low liquidity preference.

3. To which school do you subscribe—Quantity Theorist, Keynesian or Monetarist?

The essay question is obviously part of the macro-theory approach, as seen through Keynesian eyes, but the second part of the question depends on where the candidates' loyalties lie.

The effect of D > S of money?

a. *Quantity Theorist*: main result would be on *aggregate expenditure*. With a fully employed economy being assumed, households would try to obtain money holdings by reducing their expenditure on current goods and services—this might have an effect on lowering prices.

b. *Keynesian*: main result would be on the *rate of interest*. Keynes tended to simplify the picture by suggesting that the alternative to holding money was holding securities, using irredeemable government stock as a representative asset. Households would tend to acquire money holdings by selling this stock, resulting in their price falling and their yield rising. This rise in the interest rate would not have a significant effect on expenditure in the goods and services market, and they viewed the expenditure variable as interest-inelastic.

c. *Monetarist*: the main result would be on *aggregate expenditure* via *interest rates*. Modern monetarists are closer to the Keynesians in accepting what happens to a disturbance in the demand and supply of money. But they see the choice as more complex than simply money or bonds. There is a whole spectrum of assets ranging from the most liquid (money), through short- and long-term bonds, and equities to such illiquid assets as investment goods. Consumer goods were also brought into the picture as they were accorded as having a rate of return in terms of the amount of utility derived from their consumption. Not only may a person's wealth be distributed among this portfolio of assets so that the rate of return at the margin was equal for all assets, but any changes in interest would have a definite effect on aggregate expenditure. Aggregate expenditure is assumed to be highly interest-elastic with investment, house purchases and even consumer durables being influenced by changing interest rates.

Essay questions

1. *Explain the liquidity preference theory of the rate of interest.*   *(IB)*

2. *Discuss the main determinants of the rate of interest.*   *(Lond.)*

3. *Examine the view that in order to control the economy all that is required is control of the money supply.*   *(O/C Board)*

4. *What determines the level of interest rates?*   *(Oxf.)*

5. *Explain the effect of a reduction in the rate of interest on investment, income and saving in the Keynesian system and show how these changes are related.*   *(Camb.)*

6. *To what extent, if any, is the demand for money a function of the rate of interest?*   *(JMB)*

Brief comments on essay questions

Question 2

The essay can be divided into **three** sections:

1. **Introduction**: candidates must indicate the meaning of the term 'rate of interest'. It can be defined as the price which has to be paid for the loan of money, but it is important to make clear that there are many different rates of interest, which are dependent upon the length of time of the loan and the degree of risk involved. So the question must be answered by reference to the overall level of interest rates, not a particular interest rate.

   There are two distinct schools of thought as to the fundamental determinants of the rate of interest, and a fully developed essay would contain the leading elements in both explanations.

2. **Classical Theory**: this account can be labelled the 'loanable funds' theory and it rests on the proposition that the rate of interest is determined by the supply and demand for capital. Entrepreneurs demanded investment funds because they could be put to productive use, while the public were rewarded by interest payments when supplying funds.

3. **Keynesian Theory**: this account can be labelled the 'liquidity preference' theory which rests on the proposition that the rate of interest is determined by the supply and demand for money. The demand for money is influenced by the transactions, precautionary and speculative motives, while the supply of money is determined by the authorities.

   The Keynesian theory can be illustrated by a diagram or diagrams and candidates must show that they appreciate the consequences relating to the rate of interest when a change occurs in the liquidity preference schedule and in the supply of money curve.

Suggestions for further reading

Cairncross, A. K. *Introduction to Economics*. (Butterworth, 1973.)
Chapter 28
Harvey, J. *Modern Economics*. (Macmillan, 1974.) Chapter 20
Lipsey, R. G. *An Introduction to Positive Economics*. (Weidenfeld &
Nicolson, 1975.) Chapter 43
Stanlake, G. F. *Macro-Economics: An Introduction*. (Longman, 1975.)
Chapter 13
Stanlake, G. F. *Introductory Economics*. (Longman, 1971.) Chapter 19
Whitehead, G. *Economics Made Simple*. (W. H. Allen, 1974.) Chapter 18

Essay number 16

British commercial banks are required to hold minimum reserve assets equal to 12½% of their liabilities. If an eccentric millionaire who had previously kept his money in a cabin trunk now chose to deposit £1 million in notes with some bank, state, with reasons:
a. what the maximum possible increase in lending by the banking system would be;
b. why the actual increase might be less than this. (IB)

Suggested answer

a. Commercial banks, as the name implies, are joint stock companies, with the dual function of making profits for their shareholders and giving security to its depositors. The concern of a bank is to strike a balance between the competing roles of profitability and liquidity. These roles are fulfilled by banks lending money at interest, but being able to oblige their depositors who may want to withdraw cash from their accounts.

Money is a most elusive term with definitions ranging from M^1 to M^3, but most people regard money as anything which is generally acceptáble as a means of exchange. Although notes and coins are obvious candidates as a form of money, the most important money form in the UK is the bank deposit upon which cheques can be drawn.

Bank deposits originate in two ways. Firstly, customers may deposit cash in joint stock banks and receive in exchange a bank deposit. Secondly, banks may actually create bank deposits in the name of their customers. This ability to create bank deposits is restrained by the knowledge that these deposits might need to be converted into cash, involving the holding of a certain quantity of cash, or at least certain liquid or reserve assets which are capable of being quickly converted into cash.

Prior to 1971 the cash and liquidity ratios of 8% and 28% respectively were operated by banks in their attempt to fulfil their functions soundly. But since 1971 these ratios have been replaced by a reserve assets ratio of 12½% meaning that banks had to hold 12½% of their eligible liabilities in a certain specified form, namely, balances at the Bank of

England, money at call, Treasury bills, a certain proportion of commercial bills and government stock with less than one year to maturity.

Banks are then dependent on two basic criteria: the volume of reserve assets held and the size of the reserve assets ratio to which they are obliged to work. Working to a $12\frac{1}{2}\%$ reserve assets ratio means that every one unit of reserve assets can support eight units of deposit liabilities. A more precise formula can be stated so that the credit multiplier can be calculated, and thereby used when extra reserve assets are obtained:

$$\frac{1}{\text{reserve assets ratio}} \times \text{reserve assets} = \text{bank deposits}.$$

In the case of our millionaire this would mean that the extra £1 million worth of notes would support deposit liabilities of £8 million:

$$\text{i.e. } \frac{1}{\frac{12.5}{100}} \times \pounds 1\text{m} = \frac{100}{12.5} \times 1 = 8.$$

Since 1971 till money has not been regarded as a reserve asset and so the £1 million of notes will have to be converted into reserve assets before any credit creating process can function. It might be added that the bank in question would not be able to create credit and support deposit liabilities of £8 million on *its own*. Any attempt to do this would result in an inevitable drain in cash away from this bank to other banks after the clearing of cheques had taken effect. But if other banks are expanding their lending, the first bank would lend a percentage of the £1 million i.e. only seven eighths of £1 million would be loaned so that when other banks acquired deposits from members of the public, their cash balances would finally increase, thereby enabling a multibank expansion of deposit liabilities to take place to a total of £8 million.

All the banks could claim that they had not created credit, but in fact the banking system as a whole had certainly been responsible for the creation of an extra £7 million worth of money in the form of bank deposits. The balance sheets of the first bank and others collectively would appear as follows:

Bank no. 1			*Bank nos. 2, 3, 4 etc*	
Liabilities	Assets		Liabilities	Assets
£1m	£$\frac{1}{8}$m Reserve Assets		£7m	£$\frac{7}{8}$m Reserve Assets
	£$\frac{7}{8}$m Loans			£6$\frac{1}{8}$m Loans
£1m	£1m		£7m	£7m

b. The banking system is not able to create money indefinitely nor to the maximum possible extent. The reserve assets ratio is only a minimum ratio and banks may decide to hold excess reserves taking their ratio to perhaps 15%.

The banks' attitude towards profitability, particularly when interest rates are low, may result in the maximum possible increase in lending not being achieved. Much depends on the profit opportunities and perhaps the existence of uncreditworthy borrowers.

As deposit liabilities expand and with it people's incomes, there is a strong likelihood that the public will demand more cash from the banking system. This leakage of cash from the banks will reduce the credit multiplier so that the actual leakage will be magnified by a multiple of 8.

The extra £1 million worth of notes will have to be converted into reserve assets by the bank, but the percentage of them kept as till money (not a reserve asset) will have important ramifications on total deposits.

Finally, the power of the banking system to create bank deposits can be severely restricted by the Bank of England, working on behalf of the government. Since 1971 competition and credit control changes, the Bank of England has used various monetary weapons to vary the volume of reserve assets held by the banks. By using open market policy, supported by special deposits, the balances at the Bank of England can be increased or reduced so that the banks are encouraged or restricted in their ability to create credit.

Comments

A. Specific points

1. Division of the essay into **two** sections:

   a. Explanation of how banks create money.

   b. Explanation of the main limitations on banks creating credit.

   Each section should be given equal prominence with a tendency for section **a.** to be developed more fully.

2. Points of Emphasis:

   a. There is a dual role for Commercial banks in balancing profitability with security. Their ability to create bank deposits may increase the money supply.

   b. The existence of reserve assets forms a base upon which money can be created, while the credit multiplier depends upon the size of the reserve assets ratio, currently at $12\frac{1}{2}$%.

   c. A numerical example using the credit multiplier formula must be included.

   d. A single bank acting independently within a multi-bank system cannot sustain credit creation, but an entire banking system is able to increase bank credit and thereby expand the money supply.

   e. The banking system makes profit by lending money at interest to different types of borrower, but the limitations on this credit creation include the existence of leakages, excess reserves, unsuitable borrowers, the liquidity preference of the community, and the power of the Bank of England controls.

f. Do *not* fall into the trap of merely giving a list of Bank of England weapons of control. It is an important limitation on the banking system's ability to create money but it must be kept in perspective in this particular essay.

B. General points

1. Make sure that the following terms are understood:

a. fiat or token money	**e.** credit multiplier
b. fractional reserve banking	**f.** legal tender
c. reserve assets ratio	**g.** money supply
d. liabilities	**h.** near money.

2. Taking a closer look at 'money';

a. *Definition*

A simple definition might be that money is anything which is generally accepted as a means of payment, i.e. a medium of exchange. This quality of 'general acceptability' is associated with an ability to measure the value of the items exchanged, and depends on the monetary authorities regulating its supply so that people will have confidence in its purchasing power. However, money is only one among a number of other financial assets which can act as a store of value, and in inflationary times assets other than money might be the best safeguard of one's wealth.

b. *Essential Nature of Money*

It is a *perfectly liquid asset* and can be viewed as one of a whole spectrum of financial assets of varying degrees of liquidity. A financial asset other than money offers a reward to its holder but has to be balanced against the (i) risk, (ii) cost and (iii) difficulty of turning that asset into money. These assets may be held as useful stores of value but they are subject to restrictions when it comes to acting as a medium of exchange. Is it possible to place assets in a descending order of liquidity from money with its 100% liquidity to a real asset such as a house or a factory?

c. *Financial Intermediaries*

An intermediary performs the function, as the name implies, of a middle man. Financial intermediaries are no exception to this rule, and comprise institutions which borrow money from people or other institutions with surplus funds and lend it to those in search of funds. These intermediaries can be categorised as follows—

i. Banks—including clearing banks, merchant banks, discount houses, London branches of overseas banks, savings banks and National Giro.

ii. Institutional Investors—including life insurance companies, pensions funds, investment trust and unit trusts.

iii. Building societies and finance houses.

They hold assets of different types some of which are named 'quasi or near money' because although they are extremely liquid, they are not normally used as a medium of exchange, e.g. deposit accounts with banks, national savings accounts and building societies' accounts. The other assets which might be included such as Treasury bills, deposits with merchant banks and finance houses, insurance policies, unit trust units and securities, all have difficulty in being turned into cash without perhaps some considerable loss.

3. When is a liability 'money'?

If a person places cash (notes) in a bank, he is merely exchanging one asset for another. He will get a bank deposit instead, on which cheques can be drawn up to the amount of his account.

When the bank acquires the cash, the bank has an asset to the value of the notes. But the bank is also liable to pay that customer on demand in cash. Consequently when a bank receives cash it acquires an asset and a liability at the same time, which are equal in value to each other. The customer's bank deposit while being *his* asset, is the bank's liability. As the public treat their bank deposits as money, and which they feel can be transferred to others by the use of the cheque system, it is true that the liabilities of commercial banks which are debts by the banks, are in fact money.

These bank deposits can emerge by the banking system making loans, and deliberately incurring liabilities, which appear in the accounts as bank deposits—which are used by customers to pay for transactions.

All financial institutions can make loans and thereby incur liabilities but *these liabilities are not accepted by the public as money.* They do not fully offer the public a money transmission service and their obligations do not form part of the money supply. Their liabilities would be termed 'near money'.

4. What is the exact amount of money supply?

From what has been said it is obvious that the answer to the question depends on how you would define money in the first place. These days it is commonplace to accept two concepts.

a. A narrowly defined M^1 containing notes and coins in circulation plus sterling current account bank deposits in the private sector.

b. A more widely defined M^3 made up of M^1 plus all other bank accounts in the private and public sectors.

In December 1976 their total values were $M^1 = £18.5$ billion
$$M^3 = £45 \text{ billion}$$

The latter ignores accounts in non-bank institutions such as building societies, and it is interesting that a rise in interest rates on deposits at building societies might result in a movement of funds from bank deposits to the building societies, resulting in a fall in the money supply!

Essay questions

1. *Analyse how changes in the value of money affect its ability to fulfil its functions.*   *(IB)*

2. *Show how the assets of a commercial bank are distributed in accordance with the twin aims of liquidity and profitability.*   *(Lond.)*

3. *Describe the operation of the credit multiplier in a banking system. How might this be used by the central bank to control the total amount of credit available to an economy?*   *(O/C Board)*

4. *What would you include in a definition of money? How might this definition change over time?*   *(O/C Board)*

5. *Commercial bankers often assert that the banking system cannot (and does not) create money. Explain why this assertion may have some validity for each bank considered singularly, but is certainly incorrect for the banking system considered as a whole.*

 Illustrate your answer by considering the effect of an initial deposit of £10,000 in bank notes paid into an individual bank. (Assume that banks are required to observe a 10% ratio of cash to total liabilities).   *(WJEC)*

6. *What is a bank?*   *(JMB)*

Brief comments on essay questions

Question 6

This essay question is indeed open ended, thereby resulting in some confusion for many candidates. They just do not know where to start and what is expected of them. It is easier to rephrase the question so that it becomes 'what does a bank do?' or 'what are a bank's functions?' There might be a great temptation to indulge in a long list of functions of all the many types of bank operating in the UK. However examiners are trying to see if the *basic* functions of a bank are understood:

a. to accept deposits;
b. to make loans.

The nucleus of this essay must be the concentration by banks on *credit creation*. A simplified essay format might be as follows:

1. Indicate the place of the bank deposit in the money supply (the greater part of the total value of all transactions in the UK is settled by cheque payment based on bank deposits.)

2. Present the bank as a firm in the private sector attempting to balance its profit making activities with its concern for the security and liquidity of the bank. (Depositors require immediate withdrawal of their money when required, but shareholders would like to see banks making profits.)

3. With the use of the reserve assets ratio concept and a simple numerical example, candidates should explain how the credit multiplier operates.

4. Finally a balance sheet indicating the main assets and liabilities can be produced, so that one can see quite clearly that a bank is an intermediary between clients depositing money and potential borrowers using that money.

5. A conclusion might show that the money supply and the bank's functions are inextricably linked.

Suggestions for further reading

Giles, C., ed. *Understanding Economics*. (The Manchester Economics Project–Ginn & Co., 1971.) Chapter 6

Harvey, J. *Modern Economics*. (Macmillan, 1974.) Chapter 22

Lipsey, R. G. *An Introduction to Positive Economics*. (Weidenfeld & Nicolson, 1975.) Chapters 41–42

Livesey, F. *A Textbook of Economics*. (Polytech Publishers Ltd., 1978.) Chapter 12

Peters, G. H. *Private and Public Finance*. (Fontana/Collins, 1971.) Chapters 2–4

Stanlake, G. F. *Macro-economics: An Introduction*. (Longman, 1975.) Chapters 11–12

Essay number 17

How may a government attempt to control the supply of money through its
central bank? Explain the difficulties involved in the methods of
control. (CA)

Suggested answer

The supply of money is generally taken to mean the notes and coins in circulation and particularly the quantity of bank deposits in existence. While
notes and coins (currency) are under the direct control of the Bank of
England, this is not used as a means of controlling the money supply. Action lies instead with the ability of the Bank of England to affect the
lending ability of the clearing banks, as the creation of bank deposits
dominates the money supply. However the government realises that there
is no hard and fast rule between what is money and what is not money,
thereby showing the importance of credit instruments from any
institution.

In 1971 new methods of credit control were introduced which changed
previous thinking in two basic ways. All financial institutions were encouraged to compete far more, with clearing banks abandoning their
agreements on interest rates, and fixing their own base rates instead. Even
the discount houses agreed not to tender for Treasury bills collectively as
a syndicate.

Linked with this competitive urge, the banking system was to be treated
uniformally and all financial institutions were brought within the confines
of the new policy. Everyone could theoretically compete for the limited
supply of available deposits. The overall intention was to control
monetary aggregates so that the various institutions could compete
amongst themselves via the rate of interest, for a share of the total supply.
Credit was to be allocated according to its price.

After 1971 the cash and liquidity ratios were discarded and replaced by
a minimum reserve assets ratio of 12½%. All banks were expected to hold

certain specified reserve assets whose value was not below $12\frac{1}{2}\%$ of their eligible liabilities. These reserve assets included balances at the Bank of England, Treasury bills and government securities with less than one year to run, among others. The importance of these inclusions was that their supply could easily be controlled by the central bank. The ratio applied to all banks, not just clearing banks as previously, but special arrangements were made for some groups of institutions, such as finance houses, having a 10% minimum reserve assets ratio.

With the minimum reserve assets ratio as its base, the Bank of England intended to vary the quantity of eligible reserve assets held by the banks. Any reduction in these reserve assets would necessitate a reduction in total deposits by a multiple of that change, i.e. 8 times. The main instrument chosen to effect this was the traditional Bank of England weapon, open market operations, which meant the Bank of England buying or selling government securities or Treasury bills on the open market. If the money supply were to be reduced, the Bank would sell the securities and the purchasers would pay for them by cheques drawn on accounts at the commercial banks. Final settlement would result in a fall in bankers' deposits at the Bank of England, which represented a reduction in eligible reserve assets. To restore the reserve assets ratio to $12\frac{1}{2}\%$ the banks would have to resort to a multiple contraction in the level of their total deposits.

Another method the Bank uses but this time covering the entire banking system, is the call for Special Deposits. Banks are required to deposit with the Bank of England a given percentage of their eligible liabilities and although earning a rate of interest equivalent to the Treasury bill rate, they are 'frozen' and cannot be regarded as eligible reserve assets. Further restraints were imposed on the banks in the late 1970s in that they were only allowed a stated rate of growth in interest-bearing eligible liabilities over a specified period, and if the permitted level was exceeded, a proportion of the excess had to be deposited with the Bank of England in non-interest bearing Special Deposits. Calls for special deposits had the same effect as open market sales of securities.

The importance of government borrowing has meant the existence of large supplies of Treasury bills within the banking system. As this action increases the supply of reserve assets held by banks, it makes it difficult to control the overall supply of money. A policy of funding has been operated whereby the Bank of England has issued more long-term securities and fewer short-term securities or Treasury bills at the weekly tender. This enables open market policy and special deposit calls to have greater effect.

Finally, while the allocation of the credit available was intended to be controlled by market forces, the authorities still reserved the right to give qualitative guidance to the banks, and during the 1970s such advice was received by the banks in attempts to restrict lending to property developers, and to give priority to export and investment finance.

The methods of control throw up difficulties in that open market operations can only reduce the total deposits of banks if the banks are already operating with the minimum level of reserve assets. Any surplus reserve assets held by banks tend to make open market policy ineffective, and this is where funding can make the banking system more vulnerable to open market policy.

Even special deposit calls in the past were countered by the banks in that they reduced their 'investments' to accommodate this, so as to avoid squeezing their 'advances'. As the Bank of England was always prepared to buy government stock rather than let the interest rate rise, the original intention of cutting spending was not really achieved. Currently, calls for special deposits will denude the banks of reserve assets as instructions have been given that long-term securities are not to be sold in order to obtain the funds for such special deposits. In any case, since 1971 the Bank of England has notified the banking system that it will not automatically enter the gilt-edged market to maintain the price of securities at a stable level.

The attempt to carry out open market policy in Treasury bills is made almost impossible by the fact that these bills are regarded as good as cash with the Bank of England always agreeing to convert them into cash through its policy of lender of last resort. It seems the only way in which the Bank can use Treasury bills in its open market operations is to sell them to the non bank public, i.e. the institutions outside the clearing banks, so that payment for them will reduce the cash reserves of the banks without giving them a liquid asset in return.

Perhaps the major difficulty is that the Bank of England has responsibility for managing the national debt which tends to conflict with its role of implementing monetary policy. As the government has to borrow vast amounts of money, the Bank must see that the gilt edged market is stable, not prone to erratic fluctuations, and with securities being attractively priced. Any rise in the current interest rate will affect the fixed rate of interest on new issues of government stock, and this will increase the burden of servicing the very large national debt.

Operating in the gilt-edged market in this way can cause problems for the money supply, as by purchasing gilts in order to keep the price from falling, will result in an increase in the money supply. This may come at an inappropriate time when the Bank has to undertake open market sales of government stock. It seems the Bank is faced with an insurmountable dilemma.

Comments

A. Specific points

1. Division of the essay into **three** sections:

   a. Explanation of the money supply—a short paragraph.

   b. Bank of England weapons.

   c. Major difficulties of the weapons.

The last two points should be dealt with in depth, being treated separately or by linking the weapon and its weakness together.

2. Points of Emphasis:

   a. The major part of the money supply, bank deposits, can be affected by monetary policy, but the money supply as defined by the concepts M^1 and M^3, may only be part of the overall liquidity within the economy.

   b. The answer should concentrate on the post 1971 methods of controlling the money supply. The competition and credit control changes included:

      i. certain specified reserve assets;
      ii. a minimum reserve assets ratio on all banks with odd exceptions;
      iii. the use of open market policy and special deposits on the existing reserve assets;
      iv. the withdrawal of support from the gilt edged market.

   c. Monetary policy can be focused on either the money supply or the level of interest rates. Prior to 1971 the authorities tended to pay more attention to the interest rate because of its connection with the extremely large national debt. The 1971 proposals tended to shift the emphasis to controlling the money supply and allowing the limited amount of money to be allocated by the intensity of the demand for it. The price of credit (the rate of interest) was to be allowed to find its own level after the money supply had been decided upon. Monetary policy is a constant battle between the pull of the management of the national debt and the attempt by the authorities to control the money supply.

B. General points

1. Make sure that the following terms are understood:

a. minimum lending rate	e. gilt-edged market
b. open-market policy	f. lender of last resort
c. special deposits	g. moral suasion
d. funding	h. debt management.

2. Are the money supply and the level of interest rates related?

   a. The authorities can control the money supply and the level of interest rates so as to attempt to achieve the various economic objectives of full employment, stable prices, stable balance of payments and economic growth.

      But in reality these two variables cannot both be controlled at the same time. There has been enormous doubt as to the influence of these variables on the level of spending which has meant that over a period of years both a Keynesian and a monetarist influence have been mirrored in financial policy. The monetarists suggest that given the demand for money, the authorities can decide on a particular level of money supply but will have to accept a corresponding level of interest rates. However, the Keynesian view has been that to maintain a given level of interest rates the authorities must supply that quantity of money which corresponds to the given demand for money.

b. Open market policy fixes the money supply while minimum lending rate changes fix the interest rate level.

Open market policy is a dual policy involving the purchase and sale of gilt-edged securities in the Stock Exchange and Treasury bills in the discount market. This policy certainly can change the money supply but in the process, the prices of the securities will also be affected. As the security prices and security yields are inversely related, open market operations will affect the rate of interest.

At the same time the authorities attempted to create a cash scarcity in the banking system by selling Treasury bills. When the banks begin to 'call in' their money from the discount houses, the latter are forced to borrow from the Bank of England at the penal rate, Bank Rate. Gradually Bank Rate became the nucleus of a set of borrowing and lending rates so that any change in Bank Rate initiated by the Bank of England affected a whole layer of interest rates by set amounts. The minimum lending rate today follows the 'market established' Treasury bill rate and is influenced by the extent of government borrowing. However, the authorities still use open market policy and other weapons to edge up interest rates, with the minimum lending rate then following. In moments of crisis or mini-crisis the automatic formula for fixing the minimum lending rate is suspended, and the Bank of England merely changes it of its own volition.

3. Why does the Bank of England intervene in the gilt-edged market?

a. The biggest borrower in the UK today is the government. It manages to persuade institutions and the public to give up money in return for government securities, Treasury bills and an array of bonds such as defence bonds, savings certificates and premium bonds. Most of the debts have maturity dates but some are undated or irredeemable. On 31st March 1976 the national debt stood at approximately £54 billion, with over 90% of it being held by the banking sector, other financial institutions (building societies, insurance companies, pension funds), overseas holders (such as Central Banks, overseas banks, the IMF etc.), trusts (including public trustees, private funds, trusts and charities), and not forgetting the Issue Department of the Bank of England. The members of the public held only about 5% of this debt. This huge total was approximately one half of the country's national income at that time.

b. Every year about £2 billion of this debt reaches maturity and the holders require prompt payment otherwise government stock would not be regarded as 'gilt-edged'. Someone has the onerous task of trying to persuade people and institutions to buy new stock to help finance the matured stock. As if this task wasn't that difficult, there is still the current debt to service, that is, to finance the interest payments on the stock. As a final straw, the current borrowing requirement of the government for the current fiscal year has to be considered, that is, the excess of expenditure over revenue, linked with the possible high interest rate level pertaining at the time, which might make servicing the debt a real challenge in the future.

c. The British problem is more worrying due to the higher ratio of debt to national income as compared with many other countries. The British solution to the problem of how to maximise the selling of this debt is to try to achieve an 'orderly market'. The Bank of England feels that potential purchasers of this type of debt require a stable capital value for their stock. However, any fall in the price of this stock will merely lead to expectations of a further fall. The Bank of England then is not prepared to see the stock prices falling as investors would be unwilling to purchase stock in these circumstances. The authorities tend to enter the gilt-edged market and purchase stock at times of falling bond prices. This unfortunately increases the money supply as the stock is bought with a cheque drawn on the Bank of England. Thus when we have situations where interest rates are rising (or gilt-edged prices are falling) the authorities have been intervening in the gilt-edged market and purchasing bonds.

d. Since 1971 the authorities withdrew their automatic support from the gilt-edged market except on occasions of their own choosing. This move illustrated the authorities' concern over the control of the money supply rather than the management of the national debt.

Essay questions

1. *Analyse the changes which have taken place in recent years in the methods by which the Bank of England controls the commercial banks in the United Kingdom. (Lond.)*

2. *How does the Central Bank control the credit policy of the commercial banks? (Lond.)*

3. *'The minimum lending rate is the old Bank Rate in disguise'. Discuss. (O/C Board)*

4. *By what means can the Bank of England control the level of interest rates in the UK? (Oxf.)*

5. *What are the functions of the Bank of England? (JMB)*

Brief comments on essay questions

Question 5

The essay question appears straightforward, with an explanation and analysis of the main functions being expected. Most textbooks carry a long list of these functions and the candidate has the task of concentrating on the main ones within the time limit for the question. A common mistake here is for the candidate to over-emphasise a function which is fully understood to the exclusion (or near exclusion) of many of the other equally important functions.

A suggested format:

Introduction: candidates should not be tempted to indulge in a long drawn out history of the formation of the Bank of England. Concise comments only are necessary in this respect, and the position of the Bank as an intermediary between the public and private sectors must be established.

Functions:

a. It is the sole note issuing authority: explain that the entire note issue is fiduciary (backed by government securities) constituting the legal tender portion of the money supply. It must be emphasised that the ability to increase the fiduciary issue does not play a part in controlling the level of aggregate demand, and is only used to accommodate the demands of the public at certain times of the year.

b. It is the bankers' Bank: the clearing banks deposit part of their cash in an account at the Bank of England, known as Bankers' Deposits. Interbank indebtedness can be settled by using these accounts, as can withdrawals of cash, to boost till money at the banks. But the Bank of England can concentrate its monetary weapons in altering the size of Bankers' Deposits, and thereby affecting the credit potential of the clearing banks.

c. It is the government's Bank: the Bank of England holds the government's main accounts through which all current and capital expenditure and income flow. It manages the National Debt on behalf of the government and in so doing conflicts with its other role of controlling the money supply. Externally the Bank intervenes from time to time in foreign exchange markets so as to influence the exchange value of sterling.

d. It is the lender of last resort: the Bank of England lends to the short-term money market via the discount houses but often at a penal rate. It has the ability to exert pressure on interest rates throughout the money market, but always ensures that the banking system can fulfil its obligations to its customers. (This overall supervision was well illustrated in the mid 1970s when the Bank of England organised the 'lifeboat' scheme to aid many 'fringe' or secondary banks whose collapse threatened the stability of the entire banking system.)

e. It implements the monetary policy of the government: there is a grave danger here that candidates will attempt to explain in detail *all* the weapons used by the Bank of England. In the context of this essay, only the major instruments of control such as open market policy, minimum lending rate, special deposits and reserve assets ratio should be included with increased emphasis on the change in policy after 1971.

It is this last function which candidates tend to concentrate upon, and the whole array of monetary weapons are explained in great detail. While this may show the examiner complete understanding of monetary policy it does not—on its own—answer the question set. This function must be kept in perspective.

Suggestions for further reading

Giles, C., ed. *Understanding Economics.* (The Manchester Economics Project—Ginn & Co., 1971.) Chapters 6, 12

Harvey, J. *Modern Economics.* (Macmillan, 1974.) Chapter 23

Lipsey, R. G. *An Introduction to Positive Econonics.* (Weidenfeld & Nicolson, 1975.) Chapter 42

Peters, G. H. *Private and Public Finance*. (Fontana/Collins, 1976.)
 Chapter 6
Stanlake, G. F. *Macro-economics: An Introduction*. (Longman, 1974.)
 Chapters 12, 14

Essay number 18

Define inflation and explain why it is generally regarded as an evil. (JMB)

Suggested answer

The major difficulty in defining inflation is in selecting the correct definition. Some economists have stated that inflation means 'too much money chasing too few goods', while others have called it a condition of 'excess demand'. But these definitions have one thing in common and that is the terminology used suggests a possible cause and methods of controlling it.

Perhaps the most acceptable definition might be 'a persistent and sustained rise in the general level of prices' which is synonomous with a general fall in the value of purchasing power. During most years changes occur in relative prices as it is obvious that some prices must rise at different rates, while others may even fall. But inflation can only be said to occur when the average level of all prices continues to rise, and this would be indicated by some price index capable of measuring the price level, ususally the Index of Retail Prices.

Having accepted that inflation means persistently rising prices, it is customary to classify inflation as being either demand pull or cost push. The three main elements within aggregate demand are consumer spending, investment spending and government spending. When the pressure from these sources exceeds the total supplied at current prices, the price level is pulled upwards. We usually associate this type of inflation with full employment conditions so that when capacity has been reached, the pressure spills over into the factor market resulting in further price rises. Recently the source from which the excess demand arises tended to be the high level of government expenditure which, not being financed from taxation but from bank borrowing, involved an increase in the money supply.

Although cost push inflation is initiated by increases in the factor prices setting off inflationary spirals, it is common to assume that the prime factor is wage increases which are not backed by increases in productivity. Import prices and indirect taxation both play a full part in this cost push process, but it is felt that the wage price spiral is the root cause. This process does not need to be associated with an economy operating at full capacity although trade union bargaining strength is usually accepted as stronger under these circumstances. In recent years unemployment rates have been far higher without seemingly causing an abatement in wage claims.

There are grounds for stating that rising prices should be encouraged. Economic growth may respond to slowly rising prices as investment expands, and with a mild demand inflation, firms find that their current revenue exceeds their past costs. But on balance, inflation, particularly of the sort experienced in the last decade, is something to be avoided. To begin with, some sections of the population within the domestic economy are affected adversely. A rise in prices will affect the purchasing power of everyone, as the cost of living rises. The real income of the community will depend on whether a section of people have been able to expand their money income faster than the rise in prices. A redistribution of real income occurs, with certain sections gaining or losing from the process. Pensioners will tend to lose as their incomes are fixed, while strong trade unionists manage to beat the average rise in prices by militant action on wage claims. Incomes based on profits are dependent on the type of inflation being experienced as demand pull inflation will tend to look favourably on profit earners as the costs of productive factors are inclined to be more rigid than the market prices of the goods sold. Any cost inflation would tend to react badly on profit margins as the limited demand restricts an employer's ability to pass on the full burden of the costs.

Investment is essential for an economy to expand, but the finance necessary may not be forthcoming in periods of inflation, as prospective lenders of money are being penalised. Any creditors or lenders of money tend to lose as the purchasing power of money repaid to them at the end of the loan will be less than the money originally loaned. Spending not saving is encouraged and this may occur at a time when aggregate spending power is already excessive. The relative lack of saving may result in higher interest rates emerging as creditors expect additional income before they are prepared to lock their money away. These higher interest rates may have detrimental effects on the level of investment.

Inflation has repercussions on international indebtedness in that if the UK's rate of inflation exceeds that of its competitiors the UK balance of payments will move into deficit. Higher domestic price levels in the UK will discourage foreigners from buying British goods while at the same time the level of imports will rise as foreign goods are relatively cheaper than British ones. The deficit on current account is magnified if demand inflation occurs as the growth prospects imply an inward surge of imports.

It must not be forgotten that the postwar relationship between inflation and unemployment, known as the Phillips' curve connection, was not sustained during the later 1960s and 1970s, and inflation and unemployment were able to live side by side. The existence of inflationary price changes and excessive costs led to firms being priced out of domestic and foreign markets, resulting in an increase in unemployment. Stagflation became a popular cliche.

Finally, inflation's most tragic by product was the expectation of even more rapid price rises in the future. An inflationary spiral is difficult to bring under control as it is self perpetuating. Wage claims feed on price rises and people believe that the only way to beat the system is to spend early enough before the potential onset of the terrifying prospect of hyper-inflation.

Comments

A. Specific points

1. Division of the essay into **two** sections.

    a. Definition of inflation—a *brief* but clear explanation of the main causes of inflation. Candidates must not over-elaborate on this section.

    b. Effects of inflation—this will form the major part of the essay.

2. Points of Emphasis:

    a. There is a difficulty in arriving at a fully acceptable definition of inflation, because of the causal nature of many definitions.

    b. The distinction between the rival theories as to the root cause of generally rising prices—ranging from demand pull to cost push varieties. There are many more inclusions here but it would rather outweigh the essay in favour of the causes of inflation.

    c. Give at least one explanation why inflation might be regarded in a favourable light.

    d. Half a dozen separate consequences must be included in this section to give a convincing account of the disastrous repercussions of inflation.

B. General points

1. Make sure that you understand the following terms:

    a. creeping inflation   **e.** inflationary spiral
    b. imported inflation   **f.** suppressed inflation
    c. reflation   **g.** administered prices
    d. Phillips Curve   **h.** the new inflation.

2. Candidates have to make **two** important decisions:

    a. How far should one proceed with the causes of inflation? A consideration of the sources of demand is important, emphasising the connection with the capacity of a country, and the growing influence of government expenditure.

The cost push version may be dominated by the influence of trade unions but overseas influence will play a considerable part via commodity prices. An economy with excess capacity can still experience cost push inflation, even though the intensity of the wage demands is supposed to mellow with the onset of unemployment.

b. The expansion of a small number of effects or the brief inclusion of a large number of effects poses a problem.

The former viewpoint is probably most acceptable with the international scene, the domestic scene and the different categories of income receivers being to the fore.

3. Where will this inflation terminology end?

Inflation has been divided into various categories:
a. creeping **b.** galloping **c.** chronic **d.** hyper.

Inflation has been classified according to its cause:
a. wage inflation **b.** price inflation **c.** imported inflation **d.** demand inflation.

Inflation has been linked with unemployment by the use of such terms as:
a. stagflation **b.** slumpflation

Inflation is related to its opposite number by such terms as:
a. disinflation **b.** deflation **c.** recession **d.** depression

The staggering amount of verbiage leaves most candidates (and teachers) in a state of concern as to their capability in selecting the correct definition to fit the appropriate term.

4. Can a hyper-inflation ever hit the United Kingdom?

No country is completely immune from this terrible disease if its government policies are not carefully considered by its perpetrators. What happened in Germany after the First World War is frightening in its relevance for today's politicians.

In 1914 the exchange rate between the German and British currencies was £1 = 20 marks. By 1923 the British pound cost 20 billion marks. German prices had risen to such a level that a packet of cigarettes in Germany required a 1 billion mark bank note to purchase it. Prices in German shops had risen by 1,247,000 times since 1914. The Germans began to lose faith in their own currency, getting rid of as many marks as possible in exchange for either real assets or foreign currency. The government merely added to the panic by borrowing from the Reichsbank. The printing press worked overtime to such an extent that the most common currency denominations, one, ten and 100 mark notes, became literally valueless. Prices changed so rapidly that you could order a meal and see the waiter doubling the menu prices while you were enjoying your meal. People would buy anything rather than keep money.

Dr Schacht, a banker, was given the task of salvaging the mess, and began by introducing a new form of currency—the rentenmark. Even the depression throughout Europe in the early 1930s could not damage the stature of this new currency.

However the most severe inflation ever recorded occurred between 1945 and 1946 in Hungary when the new currency, the forint, replaced the old currency, the pengo, at a rate of $\frac{1}{3}$ forint = 400 octillions of pengo—a grand total of 29 noughts! (1 octillion = $1,000,000,000^3$).

5. The connection between inflation and **a.** wages **b.** savings.

a. Wages and the Phillips curve.

There is a view that postwar governments have been responsible for maintaining too high a level of spending which not only sustained full or overfull employment levels, but enabled trade unions to successfully claim higher wages without the fear that redundancies might occur as a result. Demand pull and cost push are seen to be interwoven with a definite connection seen between full employment and high inflationary rates.

This close statistical relationship was illustrated by Professor Phillips when he investigated the link between the level of unemployment and the rate of change in money wages in the UK from the mid 19th century to the 1950s. From this analysis he concluded that an unemployment rate of about $2\frac{1}{2}$% would be necessary for stable prices to emerge in the UK. The twin government objectives of full employment and stable prices were found to be in conflict, and by lowering unemployment levels the wage level was bound to rise leading perhaps to an intolerable level of inflation. This is represented by (Fig. 1) below, which indicated a downward sloping line showing a trade off between inflation and unemployment.

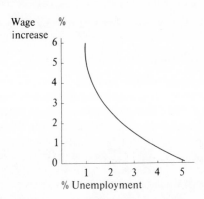

Fig. 1

This Phillips curve relationship proved an inadequate explanation of the events of the 1960s. Higher unemployment in those years did nothing to dampen wage claims. In fact there was a case for suggesting that unemployment tended to increase militancy within the trade unions. Inflation was more likely in these conditions as the lower level of demand meant that production was not utilising all the capacity, and the expensive overheads had to be covered by a rise in prices.

b. Savings and the rate of interest.

The traditional approach to savings was that while money saved would have its value eroded by the onset of 'creeping inflation' (3 or 4% p.a.) the amount of interest earned would more than offset this. In recent years we have seen record levels of interest rates and record levels of inflation rates, but inflation has won. The money rate of interest may be quite high, but the 'real' rate of interest has proved to be negative. For instance, if a person deposited £100 in a building society in 1977 and the money rate of interest was 10% the nominal total owned by that person would have risen to £110 by the end of the year. If prices had risen by 20% during 1977 the real value of the £110 would only be £91.66. This was obtained by attempting to extract the price element from the £110 by the following calculation:

$$\frac{£110}{1} \times \frac{100}{120} = £91.66.$$

When one compares the person's original £100 with its real value at the end of the year, £91.66, the effect would be that of a real interest rate which is negative, i.e. he would have lost £8.34 in real terms, a negative real interest rate of 8.34%.

Real interest rates are negative when the rate of inflation is higher than the nominal interest rates charged by most financial institutions.

Essay questions

1. *Explain why many countries have recently experienced both increasing rates of inflation and higher unemployment.* (CA)

2. *Discuss the view that restriction of the supply of money is the only effective way to check inflation.* (IB)

3. *Why is the control of inflation a common objective of government policy? What, if anything, might be said in favour of inflation?* (Lond.)

4. *Which policy measure might a government consider implementing in order to contain demand-pull inflation?* (O/C Board)

5. *'Inflation is caused by excess demand'. Discuss.* (Oxf.)

6. *'The main objection to inflation is that it involves an arbitrary redistribution of income and wealth.' Explain and discuss this statement illustrating your answer by identifying some of the main beneficiaries and victims. Indicate* briefly *other reasons why inflation might be considered undesirable.* (WJEC)

7. *Distinguish between the main types of inflation experienced in recent years, and explain why it has proved difficult to cure inflation.* (Camb.)

Brief comments on essay questions

Question 2

This is an open ended question and will give many candidates the opportunity to develop and analyse the importance of the money supply within an economy. However certain words in the question—'only', 'effective'—must direct the candidates' approach along slightly narrower lines. Some of the following points could well be used by candidates:

1. A correct interpretation of the 'money supply' is required.

2. A clear but brief analysis of the quantity theory of money could be presented with a few limitations as to its effectiveness as a theory.

3. The idea of the importance of money can be amplified by the introduction of the Friedmanite monetarist approach with its conviction that the sole cause of inflation is the excessive rise in the money supply.

4. As the term 'discuss' appears in the question, one is at liberty to suggest that other theories for containing inflation have some plausibility—incomes policy, deflationary policies, attack on government expenditure and the difficulty of overseas influences (commodity price boom).

5. The effectiveness of any theory depends upon how far the particular theory is carried—and in this respect effectiveness must be judged by the opportunity cost of achieving a low rate of inflation.

Suggestions for further reading

Cairncross, A. K. *Introduction to Economics*. (Butterworth, 1973.) Chapter 27

Giles, C., ed. *Understanding Economics*. (The Manchester Economics Project—Ginn & Co., 1971.) Chapter 12

Lipsey, R. G. *An Introduction to Positive Economics*. (Weidenfeld & Nicolson, 1975.) Chapters 43, 50–51

Harvey, J. *Modern Economics*. (Macmillan, 1974.) Chapter 28

Stanlake, G. F. *Introductory Economics*. (Longman, 1971.) Chapters 24, 25, 33

Essay number 19

Is Government borrowing inflationary? *(Oxf.)*

Suggested answer

The United Kingdom has gradually become far more of a mixed economy in that the State is playing an ever increasing role in the economic and social decision making processes of the country. No longer can we think of the State as merely fulfilling its traditional function of preserving law, order and defence, but its commitments have become wide-ranging owing to its acceptance of a series of objectives such as full employment, a reasonable growth rate and the control of inflation. It has intervened more and more in particular sectors of the economy for social and economic reasons involving huge payments of subsidies to agriculture, loans to nationalised industries and a desire to maintain the highest standards of health, education and care for the less well off. All this costs a great deal of money which must be financed in some way.

While the assortment of different types of taxation is remarkable in its diversity, the government has felt that it cannot possibly expect to raise sufficient finance by this means in case the gains of a progressive system become outweighed by the disincentive effects on work and effort.

The result has been that governments have resorted to borrowing the excess of government expenditure over taxation. This idea would have been unthinkable before the 1930s, when the principle of a balanced budget was unshakeable, but Keynesian principles infiltrated government circles to such an extent that deficit financing became perfectly permissible.

Once borrowing occurs the consequence is a rise in the National Debt which has risen from £1 million in 1694 (when the Bank of England loaned King William the vast sum of £1 million) to the astronomical figure of £54,000 million in 1976. The Bank of England is faced with the seemingly impossible task of managing this debt, that is, ensuring that the government is always able to borrow sufficient funds to redeem the maturing debt and finance current expenditure.

There are a number of sources from which funds can be obtained—the printing press, the banking system, the public and overseas. The government may resort to financing its budget deficit by allowing the printing of more bank notes which the Bank of England is entitled to do. These notes and also coins from the Mint are part of the National Debt, and originate from the Issue Department of the Bank of England, but must be balanced there by receiving an equivalent amount of securities from the government. The upshot of this borrowing from the Bank of England via the note issue is that it involves a net addition to the total supply of money and thus expenditure. The inclusion of these notes finally emerging in the asset structure of banks will enable greater credit creation and further spending, leading to possible inflation in the economy.

Although it is possible to continually finance a deficit by these means, governments are more inclined to attempt to persuade the public to accept its debt in the form of securities with varying maturity dates. As the public's money is transferred to the government there does not appear to be a net increase in expenditure. Much depends on how the public's money had originally been used. If the money had come from funds which were lying idle or hoarded, there would obviously be a net increase in spending, but if the funds borrowed had come from potential consumption, or from savings which had been invested by private industry, then an increase in government spending would have been counter-balanced by a decrease in consumption and private investment spending.

There are occasions when the government finds it difficult to persuade the public to take up all the gilts on offer. The next avenue of approach would then be the banks, and if these banks buy Treasury bills via the discount market, the increased liquidity of the banks is shown in the form of these reserve assets. On the basis of these extra reserve assets the banking system is capable of expanding credit and therefore the money supply.

Some of the National Debt may be taken up by foreigners, but although the money replacing the bonds is not part of the domestic money supply, there will be a net increase in government expenditure. To the extent that the National Debt is owned by foreigners there is the added concern that interest payments will involve a drain on the country's foreign reserves.

Finally, it has to be considered that although an increase in the money supply appears inflationary, much will depend on the overall state of the economy. An underemployed economy can absorb the increase in expenditure which occurs, giving increases in employment and real income instead of adding to the price spiral.

Comments

A. Specific points

1. Division of the essay into **two** sections.

    a. Why does the government need to borrow so much money?

    b. From whom and by what means does it finance its borrowing?

    Section **b.** should be given greater prominence and must comprise at least two thirds of the essay.

2. Points of Emphasis:

    a. There has been a tremendous expansion in government expenditure which has led to a rise in the public sector borrowing requirement. This expands the National Debt and carries with it a 'burden' on either the present or future generations.

    b. There is a firm link established between the PSBR and the potential increase in the money supply.

    c. Any money supply increase depends upon:

      i. sources of funds;
      ii. methods of finance.

    d. The main sources are the non-bank public, foreigners, and the banking system.

    e. The main methods are by issuing gilt-edged stock and/or Treasury bills.

B. General points

1. Make sure that you understand the following terms:

    a. PSBR   **d.** National Debt
    b. M^1 and M^3 **e.** public goods
    c. domestic credit expansion   **f.** budget deficit.

2. How important is public expenditure?

    a. Who are the spending agents?
      i. central government
      ii. local authorities
      iii. public corporations.

    b. What is the size of public expenditure?
      The public sector accounts for approximately one-third of the nation's capacity, and its total spending has been growing rapidly relative to private spending. In 1976 public expenditure was 60% of the Gross Domestic Product, with the central government being responsible for over one-half of the total, the other two sections covering one-quarter each.

c. Where do the funds come from?:
The two main sources are:

i. taxation
ii. borrowing (PSBR was £11 billion in 1976).

Both methods of fund raising have questionable advantages, but they may pose a threat in the constant battle over inflation and unemployment.

d. How is the money spent?
Some elements of public expenditure will:

i. make use of resources which would have gone into private use. These resources are pre-empted for public use, and while spending money on defence projects may well give some people employment, it does withdraw resources from potential private use utilising them in the public interest.

ii. transfer money from the private sector back to different people or firms within the private sector in the form of social security benefits, subsidies and grants. This latter category is a redistribution of income and has gradually become a more important element in total public expenditure.

3. To what extent does the PSBR affect the money supply and interest rates?

The PSBR is financed mainly by **a.** the sale of gilts to the public—with a forcing up of interest rates; **b.** the sale of Treasury bills mainly through the banking system—with an expansion of the money supply.

a. The sale of gilts to the public by the government will result in a fall in bond prices and a rise in the yield, but if the current level of interest rates is high the government would have to issue this new debt with a higher fixed interest rate attached. This would result in a discouragement to private investment and would further involve the authorities in increasing taxation to finance these extra interest payments. Increased taxation will also reduce disposable income and may add to the disincentive effects of taxation.

The government therefore would prefer a relatively low level of interest rates, and this has been the pattern since the MLR had been at its peak in October 1976. The immediate causes of this falling interest rate or rising bond price level were the strong buying of bonds by the institutions (insurance companies, pension funds and banks) and the surge of funds into this country from abroad coinciding with a rebirth of confidence in sterling.

Selling gilts would undoubtedly have an effect on the interest rate which the government would not look on with any favour. Governments might respond in a number of ways:

i. a reduction in government spending;
ii. an increase in taxation to finance more of the debt;
iii. peg interest rates by the government purchasing bonds in the open market—thereby increasing the money supply;
iv. advise banks to reduce loans to the private sector so that they can take up more public sector lending.

b. Government borrowing by selling Treasury bills to the banking system will finally expand the money supply many times over. Assume that the government
decided to spend £1 million and raised the money by borrowing £1 million from
the banks via Treasury bills. The following stages in the story can be followed:

   i. The banks pay £1 million for the Treasury bills from their Bankers' Deposits
   at the Bank of England. The banks have exchanged £1 million of cash (or
   balances at the Bank of England) for £1 million of Treasury bills. One type
   of reserve asset has been exchanged for another type of reserve asset, and so
   no change has taken place in the money supply.

   ii. The government spend £1 million by such means as increasing family
   allowances, widows' pensions, or old age pensions. After this money has
   been spent by the public on such items as food, heating and shelter with the
   odd luxury thrown in, the recipients of that spending might place their cash
   in their banks thereby acquiring an equal amount of bank deposits. At this
   stage the money supply has increased by the full amount of those bank
   deposits.

   iii. The banks can now indicate a position where they have the same amount of
   cash as they had before, but they have also acquired £1 million extra
   Treasury bills and £1 million extra bank desposits (this latter item showing
   an increase in the money supply).

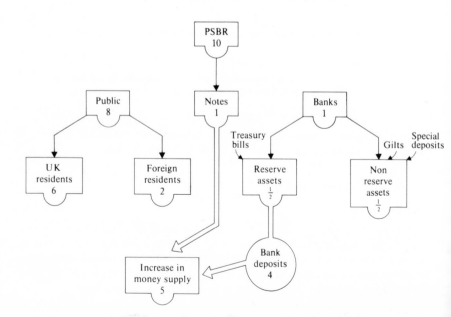

Fig. 1

    iv. With the extra £1 million of Treasury bills (reserve assets) the banks can make new loans to the extent of an *extra* £7 million (with a 12½% reserve assets ratio). When the borrowers spend this money by means of drawing a cheque, the recipients tend to pay these cheques into their bank accounts and thus bank deposits are increased.

    v. If we include the previous £1 million bank deposits, the total amount of bank deposits created would be £8 million, all on the basis of a release of £1 million of Treasury bills from the bank of England.

4. Does the public sector borrowing requirement affect the money supply?

    a. If the PSBR is financed by the public there will be no increase in the money supply.

    b. If the PSBR is financed by the banking system there will be an increase in the money supply if the banks take up reserve assets. (See diagram opposite.)

Essay questions

    1. *Do you consider that the existence of a National Debt is a burden upon the economy?   (IB)*

    2. *Why has the UK's public sector borrowing requirement risen in recent years? Does it matter?   (Oxf.)*

    3. *What would be the effect on the supply of money of each of the following:*

        a. *an open market sale of government securities to the public;*

        b. *the release of the 'special deposits' held at the Bank of England;*

        c. *an increase in government expenditure financed by the sale of Treasury bills to the discount houses?*

    Give a brief explanation of your answer in each case.   (WJEC)

    4. *Is the National Debt a burden to the economy?   (JMB)*

Brief comments on essay questions

Question 1

Some confusion often arises over seeing the National Debt as the nation's debt in terms of the balance of payments deficit. The term must be defined and explained in terms of its size and method of finance. Valuable time must not be spent in listing the component of the debt with details as to their ownership. A history of the National Debt is not required.

Suggested format of essay:

Introduction: a few paragraphs only on the connection between a budget deficit and government borrowing. This might include the origin of the borrowed funds in terms of the public, the banking system and foreigners.

The Burden: the major part of this essay should attempt to analyse the following points:

i. Comparison of private and public debt—the former involves a loss of resources when repayment has to be made of a debt; the latter involves a transfer of resources from one section of the community to another section of the same community.

ii. Foreign held debt—interest payments and final repayments have to be paid in foreign currency—which is scarce. Part of the nation's resources have to go in exports for this payment to be made and thus potential consumer goods in the home market will have to be sacrificed.

iii. Current versus future consumers—as long as future generations can find sufficient money to service the debt via interest payments, the current consumers are faced with the burden of the debt in as much as the opportunity cost of spending money on government schemes must be the alternatives which the current community will have to forgo in terms of reduced consumer goods.

iv. Disincentive effects—servicing the debt by increasing progressive taxation will result in less effort and therefore less output with the whole community being worse off. Any increase in taxation revenue may result in an inequitable redistribution of income if the money flows from lower income groups to wealthier bond holders.

Suggestions for further reading

Lipsey, R. G. *An Introduction to Positive Economics*. (Weidenfeld & Nicolson, 1975.) Chapter 40

Livesey, F. *A Textbook of Economics*. (Polytech Publishers Ltd, 1978.) Chapter 11

Harvey, J. *Modern Economics*. (Macmillan, 1974.) Chapter 29

Peters, G. H. *Private and Public Finance*. (Fontana/Collins, 1976.) Chapter 8

Stanlake, G. F. *Macro-economics: An Introduction*. (Longman, 1975.) Chapter 9

Stanlake, G. F. *Introductory Economics*. (Longman, 1971.) Chapter 30

Essay number 20

'Comparative cost does not fully explain international trade.'
Discuss.   (O/C Board)

Suggested answer

The basis of international trade depends upon the differences in production conditions found throughout the world. This is reflected in comparative differences in costs, thereby allowing trade to be mutually beneficial to all parties.

Resources are unevenly distributed between countries so that vast tracts of fertile land in some countries can be compared with the desert land of others. Climatic differences imply that no country can be self-sufficient in this modern age, so that trade can bring an enormous variety of goods to a country. Other countries possess resources but in quite different proportions, so that it would pay to produce goods bearing a high proportion of relatively abundant resources, because it is cheaper.

The immobility of these factors will be instrumental in the continuation of these different cost conditions between countries, a state of affairs perpetuated by migration restrictions, exchange controls and language barriers. It is the cost differences which persuade countries to specialise on those goods for which they are best suited, exchanging them for goods which other countries concentrate upon.

The explanation of comparative costs can be seen most clearly if a simplified model is analysed. Assume that there are only two countries capable of producing only two goods with a complete absence of trade restrictions and transport costs. Each country has an identical quantity of resources which can be easily transferred to the production of either good without incurring economies or diseconomies of scale.

Take the case of two countries each with an absolute advantage in the production of one good, while using the same volume of resources. The table will illustrate this relationship, with each country devoting half its resources to each good.

	Good X		Good Y
Country A	5	and	1
Country B	1	and	5

Before any thoughts of specialisation, total world production would be 6X and 6Y. But one can easily see that country A would be better employed if it specialised on good X, while country B should concentrate on good Y. After specialisation the net result would be 10X and 10Y which is certainly an overall gain in production. However, the countries cannot be said to have gained unless these goods are traded between them to their mutual advantage.

Any specialisation involves an opportunity cost element, so that in country A the opportunity cost of producing 1X will be $\frac{1}{5}$Y, while in country B the opportunity cost of producing 1X would be 5Y. Both countries have to agree on a rate of exchange which will be mutually advantageous. Country A will not be prepared to accept anything less than $\frac{1}{5}$Y for 1X, while country B will not be prepared to offer more than 5Y to obtain 1X. The actual rate will have to fall between the opportunity cost ratios of the two countries for trade to take place. If the exchange rate settles at 1X = 2Y, with country A giving up 2X to country B, in return for 4Y, the following table would result.

	Good X		Good Y
Country A	8	and	4
Country B	2	and	6

Both countries have benefited from specialisation and trading with each other, compared with the pre-specialisation position.

It is not quite so obvious that a country should trade with another if it has an absolute advantage over the other country in both goods. But if there is a comparative advantage in producing a commodity that country will specialise in that product and trade with its rival for the other product. The main criterion is that there should be a difference in the opportunity costs of producing the goods within each country. The following example may illustrate this, but it is not immediately obvious that total output has expanded after specialisation because one of the products has increased while the other has decreased. World production before specialisation is 3X and 5Y, but after specialisation with country A concentrating on good X the picture becomes 4X and 4Y—a gain in X but a loss in Y.

	Good X		Good Y
Country A	2	and	3
Country B	1	and	2

In the example the opportunity cost ratios are $1:1\frac{1}{2}$ in country A and

1 : 2 in country B, indicating that in terms of resources given up it is more meaningful for country A to specialise on X, and country B on Y. As long as the two countries specialise and the terms of trade fall within the limits of their opportunity cost ratios, both countries will gain by trading.

Since resources are scarce they have to be used in an optimum manner, and the existence of relative cost differences allow specialisation linked with exchange to maximise the total output. However, the comparative cost thesis does not fully govern the production pattern of all countries as the real world contains obstacles to complete freedom to trade. Transport costs and tariffs along with other artificial restrictions can limit the potential gains coming from the specialisation on a particular good. Countries may decide that it is more profitable to produce the good themselves even though it is obvious that another country is better equipped to deal with it.

The decision to specialise depends on the different opportunity cost ratios in the countries concerned, but as resources are utilised and concentrated on a particular product there is a distinct likelihood of diminishing returns setting in from the use of less efficient resources, and the possible existence of some fixed factor within the industry in question. This leads to an alteration in the opportunity cost ratio within that country leading to a reduction in the gains from specialisation. The existence of economies of scale as production expands may well result in a further widening in the cost differences between the countries, thereby maintaining the advantages already achieved.

The comparative cost theory cannot explain the existence of trade unless the terms of trade are mutually beneficial to interested parties. For this to happen they must lie within the limits imposed by the differing opportunity cost ratios. In the real world the terms of trade do not remain constant because the demand for products is frequently changing. Specialisation on a product which increases its output may well lead to a fall in demand and price for that product. This inevitably weakens the terms of trade in the country producing that product until it will not pay to specialise further.

Finally, countries may consider the dangers, political and economic, of being placed in a position of being too dependent on foreign trade. World conditions are frequently changing and an over emphasis on any one industry may put that country in a great deal of jeopardy.

Comments

A. Specific points

1. Division of the essay into **three** sections

   a. Fundamental basis for international trade is the uneven distribution of factors or production throughout the world, and their relative immobility—a short but clear paragraph or two will suffice.

   b. Explanation of the law of comparative costs.

c. Reasons why the law does not give a complete account of the pattern of trade.

Parts **b.** and **c.** should contain the major elements of the answer.

2. Points of Emphasis

   a. Factors of production are:

      i. unevenly distributed;
      ii. differently combined in producing a good;
      iii. immobile between countries.

   b. Different products require the use of different resources in different proportions. Country A will concentrate upon goods which embody relatively abundant and cheap resources and exchange them for goods which may embody relatively abundant resources in country B.

   c. Explanation of the law of comparative costs by utilising a hypothetical model world:

      i. two countries each with an absolute advantage over the other in the production of one good;
      ii. two countries with one of them having an absolute advantage over the other in the production of both goods, but a relative or comparative advantage in one of the goods.

   d. An analysis of the opportunity cost ratios within each country showing that trade is potentially profitable for both countries as long as the opportunity cost ratios are different.

   e. The rate of exchange of the goods must lie somewhere between the limits of the opportunity cost ratios for both countries to have a mutual advantage.

   f. The gains from specialising and trading are diminished somewhat by the existence of a number of factors which tend to narrow the opportunity cost differences:

      i. tariffs and transport costs;
      ii. opportunity cost ratios are altered by the onset of diminishing returns;
      iii. terms of trade will alter according to changes in demand and therefore prices until they no longer fall between the opportunity cost ratios.
      iv. the vulnerability of a country over specialising.

B. General points

1. Make sure you understand the following terms

   a. opportunity cost ratio   d. terms of trade
   b. absolute advantage   e. rate of exchange
   c. comparative advantage   f. specialisation.

2. Many candidates find the following distinctions most confusing:

a. What is the distinction between absolute and comparative advantage?

Some candidates experience great difficulty in selecting the particular good upon which a country should specialise. There appear to be *two* completely different methods used by candidates in arriving at their answer. This example illustrates the production possibilities of two countries utilising identical quantities of resources, distributing the resources equally between both goods.

	Good X		Good Y
Country A	4	and	1
Country B	2	and	4

Method Number One. Some candidates begin by comparing the output levels of one good produced by the two countries. In this example they can see that country A is twice as efficient as country B in the production of good X, while country B is four times as efficient as country A in the production of good Y. Country A has an absolute advantage over B in the production of good X, while country B has an absolute advantage over A in the production of good Y. This is an easy example to analyse, but it might have been more difficult if different figures were introduced.

Method Number Two. Candidates should investigate the opportunity cost, in a particular country, of producing a unit of one of the goods, then compare it with the opportunity cost of producing a similar unit of the same good in the other country. In the previous example the opportunity cost of producing 1X in country A is $\frac{1}{4}$Y, while the opportunity cost of producing 1X in country B is 2Y. The figures show that country A has a comparative advantage in the production of X because country A gives up only $\frac{1}{4}$Y for 1X compared with giving up 2Y in country B. A similar conclusion can be reached with country B having a comparative advantage in the production of Y, because country B sacrifices only $\frac{1}{2}$X for an extra Y compared with giving up 4X in country A.

The above example shows the concept of an absolute advantage of both countries in their respective goods, and a comparative advantage of both countries in their particular goods.

Another example which is more common, but more difficult to comprehend, is of a country being more efficient than another in the production of *both* goods, yet having a comparative advantage in one of them.

	Good X		Good Y
Country A	3	and	5
Country B	2	and	4

If method number one is used in this case, many candidates will not be able to assess, at a glance, as to which goods the countries will specialise upon. It is not easy to see if and where the comparative advantage lies.

It is far more reliable to use method number two, so that in country A the opportunity cost of producing 1X is $1\frac{2}{3}$Y, while in country B the opportunity cost of producing 1X would be 2Y. This leads to the conclusion that country A should specialise on good X, country B specialising on good Y. By comparing like with like candidates have been able to indicate that the movement of resources from good Y to good X will involve a smaller sacrifice if it is only completed in country A.

b. What is the distinction between the terms of trade and the domestic opportunity cost ratios?

Two important criteria have to be accepted for countries to find it profitable to trade:

i. the domestic opportunity cost ratios must be different;
ii. the terms of trade must lie within the limits set by these ratios.

Using the example quoted previously, it can be seen that country A will specialise on good X producing 6X, and country B will concentrate all its resources on good Y producing 8Y. Both countries will require exchange to take place and will finally have to agree on an acceptable rate of exchange, if there are to be mutual gains. The question comes down to the intensity of demand for the other country's good. Country A's position surely must be that it is *not* prepared to accept less than $1\frac{1}{3}$Y for a unit of X, because it could achieve $1\frac{1}{3}$Y itself by transferring resources domestically from X to Y. Therefore country A would like more than $1\frac{1}{3}$Y if only country B would agree. Country B's position is that it is *not* prepared to give up more than 2Y for every unit of X exchanged for similar reasons.

Unless the rate of exchange falls somewhere between $1X = 1\frac{1}{3}$Y or 2Y it will pay a country to move its factors out of specialised occupations and produce the good internally. The actual exchange rate will be dependent on the international market forces of supply and demand. If the demand for X from country B is greater than the demand for Y from country A, the final rate of exchange will lie nearer $1X = 2$Y than $1X = 1\frac{1}{3}$Y, for instance $1X = 1.99$Y.

Essay questions

1. *'The reasons for the division of labour are fully explained by the theory of comparative costs'. Discuss.   (Lond.)*

2. *The following table shows the price of a unit of textiles and a unit of steel in two hypothetical countries A and B, in an initial situation where no international trade takes place.*

	Textiles	Steel
Country A	£2.5	£5
Country B	$4	$16

If trade now becomes possible, show that potential gains from trade exist and indicate the likely specialisation of each country. What factors tend to restrict the degree of international specialisation in practice?   (WJEC)

3. *In two countries the total man days of labour required to produce various commodities is as follows:*

Country	Wheat per kilo	Barley kilo	Wool kilo	Iron kilo	Shoes pair	Perfume gramme	Watches 100	Cars each	Cloth metre
A	50	80	100	200	8	10	4	40	6
B	30	40	90	180	8	2	3	20	4

a. *Which two of these commodities is country A most likely to export to country B?*
Give reasons for your answer and outline the assumptions on which it is based.

b. *Explain what bearing this cost information has on the determination of the exchange rate of the currencies of country A and country B.* *(JMB)*

Suggestions for further reading

Cairncross, A. K. *Introduction to Economics.* (Butterworth, 1973.) Chapter 31

Giles, C., ed. *Understanding Economics.* (The Manchester Economics Project—Ginn & Co., 1971.) Chapter 7

Lipsey, R. *An Introduction to Positive Economics.* (Weidenfield & Nicolson, 1975.) Chapter 44

Harvey, J. *Modern Economics.* (Macmillan, 1974.) Chapter 30

Stanlake, G. F. *Introductory Economics.* (Longman, 1971.) Chapter 26

Whitehead, G. *Economics Made Simple.* (W. H. Allen, 1974.) Chapter 21

Essay number 21

What determines the Rate of Exchange between two countries?   *(WJEC)*

Suggested answer

National currencies are only completely acceptable within the confines of each nation and any transaction between nations involves a preliminary sale of one currency and the purchase of another before the good or service can be finally exchanged. The market place for such transactions in currencies is known as the foreign exchange market; with foreign exchange referring to the currency of any overseas country. Sterling is regarded as foreign exchange to a German. Clients, resident or non-resident of the UK, instruct brokers who are authorised commission agents, to contact the market with an order for currencies. The market itself comprises over two hundred and fifty institutions such as overseas branches of clearing banks, merchant banks and the London branches of the foreign and overseas banks. The banks are connected nationally and internationally with other banks in major cities by an elaborate system of telephone, telex and cable.

The rate of exchange of a currency is nothing more alarming than its price in terms of the foreign currency being exchanged for it. This price will be determined, like the price for any other commodity in a free market, by the combined forces of demand and supply. The movement of goods, services and capital between countries will all be related to the demand for and supply of a currency resulting in the external value of the currency changing from day to day. Assuming that the two countries in question are the UK and the USA, one could draw a demand and supply curve for sterling. A demand for British goods from the USA will generate a demand for sterling which will be higher, the lower the price of sterling becomes. A demand for American goods from the UK will generate a demand for dollars and consequently a supply of sterling to buy those dollars. The lower the exchange rate the more expensive imports become resulting in a decrease in demand for those imports and the dollars which would have bought them. The amount of sterling necessary to buy these dollars would therefore also decline with the supply curve for sterling tending to slope upwards from left to right.

It can be seen in Fig. 1 that under freely floating exchange rates, the rate of exchange between sterling and dollars will rest at £1 = $3.

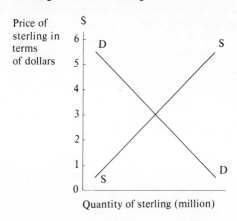

Fig. 1

However, the rate will alter if there is an increase or decrease in the demand for sterling, or an increase or decrease in the supply of sterling. In the real world a rise in tariffs on UK imports will make these goods more expensive resulting in a decrease in demand for them and therefore a decrease in the supply of sterling being offered. Probably the most important factor is the relationship between domestic price levels in the respective countries. If the UK's inflationary rate is higher than the USA's, British goods become less competitive and imports become relatively cheaper, resulting in an increase in the demand for dollars, i.e. increase in the supply of sterling, and a fall in the demand for sterling. This will shift the demand and supply curves for sterling so that eventually the rate of exchange will depreciate until it reaches a new equilibrium level. Another important factor must be the expansion in a country's money income which is bound to affect the import intake particularly if the marginal propensity to import is high. Such an expanding income might also find that potential exports are being sucked into the prosperous home market. Profit-earning prospects and changes in the rate of interest will certainly affect short- and long-term capital movements which in themselves generated a demand for or supply of sterling. Taxation policy at home and more profitable prospects abroad may combine to increase movements of investment capital overseas in the form of purchasing factories or equities. Taking advantage of higher interest rates and the threat of more inflationary wage claims can also lead to speculation and short-term movements of 'hot money' overseas. Finally, even changes in government policy towards spending overseas and political incidents such as assassinations have an effect on the relative values of currencies.

Although the pound has been allowed to float since 1972, the postwar period has seen the rate of exchange fixed within certain limits as laid down by the conditions of the IMF. The UK announced an 'official' parity in terms of dollars and the EEA assisted in maintaining that rate when it moved to within 1% either side of this parity. This can be illustrated in Fig. 2 by seeing that an increase in imports over exports would result in an increase in the demand for dollars, i.e. an increase in the supply of sterling as shown by S^1. Under normal circumstances the exchange rate would depreciate and the authorities would be obliged to restrain its progress downwards. The EEA would have to purchase sterling in the foreign exchange market so as to maintain the rate at its correct parity—as shown by the curve D^1.

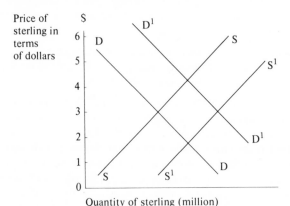

Fig. 2

The 2% band was later changed to $4\frac{1}{2}$% in 1971 so that countries would not need to use their reserves so frequently. If it was felt that a particular currency was over valued and that internal measures to bring about equilibrium in the balance of payments had been exhausted, a country might resort to changing its parity to a new and lower one, with the added assistance of the EEA again in attendance.

This abortive attempt to realign the exchange rates of the major world currencies at the Smithsonian Conference in 1971 was followed by a series of 'floats', including the UK in 1972. Since that time the practice of 'dirty floating' has increased, whereby countries with no official parity to maintain, allow their monetary authorities to intervene in the foreign exchange market to keep rates at a higher or lower level than market forces would demand.

The factors affecting the rate of exchange between two currencies are therefore an amalgamation of the forces of supply and demand with the watchful eye of the monetary authorities being ever mindful of the difficulties and dangers of particular levels of that rate.

Comments

A. Specific points

1. Division of the essay into **two** main sections

    a. A theoretical explanation of how a rate of exchange can be affected by demand and supply followed by the factors affecting that demand and supply.

    b. An explanation of how an exchange rate can be altered by the authorities.

    More time should be given to the theoretical explanation involved in section **a.**, and candidates should not fall into the trap of merely listing the factors that can affect the rate of exchange.

2. Points of Emphasis

    a. The rate of exchange is the price of a currency, just the same as the price of many other commodities, with its sphere of operations seen as the foreign exchange market.

    b. There is always a *reason* behind the purchase or sale of a currency—it is a good example of the concept of 'derived demand', e.g. the demand for dollars is derived from the demand for American motor cars.

    c. *Any* transaction, from the demand for Scottish whisky by the French to the desire to see the sights of Switzerland by a British tourist, will affect the demand/supply of a currency. Anything which affects *any* of the items involved in the balance of payments accounts will affect the rate of exchange between sterling and other currencies.

    d. Care must be paid to the diagram which is essential in this essay in indicating a candidate's understanding of the opposing forces of demand and supply. Although British exports generate a demand for sterling, with British imports generating a demand for dollars, the pressures can be seen as demand for sterling equalling a supply of dollars, with a demand for dollars equalling a supply of sterling. A careful logical analysis of their connections will pay enormous dividends.

    e. The underlying factors affecting goods, services and capital movements include such items as inflationary rates within countries; levels of income; changing rates of interest; speculation encouraged by falling reserves, threats of devaluation etc.; fiscal changes affecting the earning potential of investment projects; even the utterances of distinguished economists like Milton Friedman on the capabilities (or lack of them) of Britain's growth prospects.

    f. A fixed exchange rate system with possibilities for altering these rates through devaluation or revaluation, was the normal state of affairs prior to 1971. The difficulties of managing those rates and the pressure placed on reserves and on the domestic economy, led finally to the eventual breakdown of the IMF system, which saw attempts to patch it up.

    g. The present position is one of a floating exchange rate system with authorities attempting to manipulate the rate, protecting it from the pressures of market forces.

B. General points

1. Make sure you understand the following terms

   a. revaluation   **e.** exchange equalisation account
   b. depreciation   **f.** gold exchange standard
   c. foreign exchange   **g.** flexible exchange rates
   d. derived demand   **h.** crawling peg.

2. Points of Confusion on the Rate of Exchange

   a. What is the 'effective exchange rate'?
   With most of the major currencies now floating it is extremely difficult to arrive at a clear average value of a particular currency. Any pair of floating currencies will see their value change frequently but if one of the currencies is compared to its Smithsonian parity it will give a more accurate assessment of the change in its value. The complex calculation involves comparing how much it would cost to buy a bundle of the major currencies, the number of units of each currency bought being determined by the relative importance of trade between the two countries involved. The answer indicates how much a particular currency had depreciated or appreciated from its Smithsonian value.

   b. How do authorities intervene in the exchange rate mechanism?
   The concept of 'dirty floating' is another name for steadying the market for sterling and can be implemented in three ways:

   i. The EEA can be used along with further borrowed foreign currencies to prop up the rate. In this case the authorities are doing nothing more than buying up the sterling that is being sold in the foreign exchange market with their UK gold and foreign currency reserves. It is an expensive way of maintaining a particular rate of exchange, especially if that rate still continues to fall through the excessive sale of sterling.

   ii. The authorities may raise domestic interest rates heralded by a rise in the minimum lending rate. This enables short-term capital movements to move in the direction of the UK as the interest rate differential has been changed in its favour. Capital may move from centres where interest rates are lower to centres where the placement of short term funds can earn a larger profit. An American company may transfer a bank deposit from dollars into sterling, or might even buy British gilt-edged stocks.

   c. What is the basic difference between fixed and floating exchange rates?
   Many economists consider that the most important difference between the two theories is that:

   i. In a fixed rate system any pressure on the balance of payments which is transferred to the rate of exchange will adversely affect the volume of reserves of foreign currency held by the deficit country. As the country is obliged to maintain the rate of exchange by the use of the funds in the EEA, any continual deficit will exhaust those funds and perhaps lead to further borrowing from institutions such as the IMF.

ii. In a freely floating rate system, the pressure of a balance of payments deficit is taken by the rate of exchange, its level finally depreciating. As there is no necessity to maintain the rate at required levels, the important currency reserves can be protected, while domestic policies can be initiated to readjust the external position. However the fall in the exchange rate will only bring about equilibrium if the Marshall-Lerner condition of elasticity is satisfied (the sum of the elasticities of demand for imports and exports must be more than unity).

3. The changing fortunes of the Exchange Rate

a. *Gold Standard* (from the mid 19th century to 1931—apart from the period 1914 to 1925)
    i. Fixed exchange rates within limits set by gold points.
    ii. Convertibility of currency into gold–link between money supply and gold.

b. *The Thirties* (1931–1939)
    i. UK left the gold standard in 1931.
    ii. The rate of exchange was allowed to float.
    iii. Convertibility of currency into gold was abandoned.

c. *The Bretton Woods System* (1945–1971)
    i. Fixed exchange rates within limits set by the IMF.
    ii. It was a gold exchange standard (USA agreed to convert dollars held by foreign monetary authorities into gold at \$35 an ounce).
    iii. Adjustable peg system involved devaluation or revaluation of the currency.

d. *The Smithsonian Agreement* (1971)
    i. A realignment of exchange rates, with fixed rates within wider limits.
    ii. It was a dollar standard (central banks were told that USA had suspended convertibility of dollars into gold).

e. *The Current Position*
The major part of the western world allow their currencies to float—dirty floating.

Essay questions

1. *Why should alterations in exchange rates ever be necessary?* *(O/C Board)*

2. *What do you understand by the term 'flexible' or 'floating' exchange rates? What are the disadvantages of 'flexible' exchange rates?* *(CA)*

3. *Discuss the relative merits of fixed and floating exchange rate systems.* *(IB)*

4. *Would a floating exchange rate help to remedy an adverse balance of payments?* *(Lond.)*

5. *Discuss the relative merits of fixed and variable foreign exchange rates.* *(JMB)*

Brief comments on essay questions

Question 2

This may seem to be an opportunity for some candidates to show how much they know regarding exchange rates in general and the gold standard in particular, but the good candidate will answer the question as set.

Suggested format for essay

Definition:	(1) Exchange rate is a price.
	(2) Rate is determined by the market forces of supply and demand.
Diagram:	(1) Explanation of the main curves on the diagram.
	(2) A short explanation as to how an excessive demand for pounds will affect the exchange rate.
Comparison:	(1) Brief definition of what a fixed exchange rate system means.
	(2) Explanation of the use of the EEA to maintain the rate (this section is included to convince the examiner that the *two* systems are understood).
Disadvantages:	(1) Exchange rates may fluctuate excessively creating uncertainty in the eyes of firms and investors, and leading to a fall in investment and trade.
	(2) Speculative action can add to the instability of the rate. However a case can be made out for speculators smoothing out exchange rate variations.
	(3) The rate of inflation may be increased as a depreciation of the currency can raise the cost of imports. This may lead to militant wage demands in order to maintain living standards. A wage price spiral may take off. The inelastic nature of demand for many of the UK imports can exaggerate this inflationary tendency.

Suggestions for further reading

Cairncross, A. K. *Introduction to Economics.* (Butterworth, 1973.) Chapter 33

Giles, C., ed. *Understanding Economics.* (The Manchester Economics Project—Ginn & Co., 1971.) Chapter 20

Lipsey, R. G. *An Introduction to Positive Economics.* (Weidenfeld & Nicolson, 1975.) Chapter 45

Livesey, F. *A Textbook of Economics.* (Polytech Publishers Ltd, 1978.) Chapter 15

Harvey, J. *Modern Economics.* (Macmillan, 1974.) Chapter 32

Stanlake, G. F. *Macro-economics: An Introduction.* (Longman, 1975.)
    Chapter 18
Whitehead, G. *Economics Made Simple.* (W. H. Allen, 1974.) Chapter 23

Essay number 22

'Devaluation worsens the terms of trade and is therefore harmful'.
Discuss. (Lond.)

Suggested answer

A country will only trade if there are clear gains from doing so, and these gains are dependent on the terms of trade facing that country. The terms of trade reflect the rate at which a country's goods exchange against those of other countries, that is, the quantity of exports which must be given up in order to obtain a given quantity of imported goods. As the real world includes an enormous range of goods it is customary to show the terms of trade of a country in the form of an index number which has itself been calculated from the index of export prices and the index of import prices.

Based on the formula:

$$\frac{\text{index of export prices}}{\text{index of import prices}} \times 100,$$

any relative movement in export and import prices will affect the terms of trade, making it favourable or adverse. For example, a fall in export prices, other things remaining constant, will mean an adverse movement in the terms of trade as a given quantity of imports can now only be obtained by the country having to expand its volume of exports.

Countries undergoing balance of payments' problems and operating a fixed exchange-rate system may finally decide, after the unsuccessful use of other measures, to devalue their currency. This is usually regarded as an emergency measure and constitutes a lowering of one's currency from one fixed parity to another fixed parity.

This lowering of the exchange rate may be seen as a deliberate worsening of the terms of trade as exports are made cheaper in terms of the foreign currency while imports are made dearer in terms of the home currency. Domestic prices in both countries will not have changed but the exchange-rate adjustment will hopefully bring about quantity changes in exports and imports sufficient to improve the balance of payments' position.

There is no doubt that if the terms of trade deteriorate, with the quantities of exports and imports remaining unchanged—as they might do in the short tun—the visible balance will deteriorate also. What is important is what happens to foreign earnings and receipts after the devaluation. This will be dependent in the main on the relationship between the elasticity of demand for the country's exports and imports.

If the elasticity of demand for a country's exports was greater than unity, a fall of 5% in export prices would result in an increase in the demand for exports of greater than 5%. Foreign earnings would expand. However, the devaluation would also affect the demand for imports and the 5% increase in import prices would result in a greater than 5% fall in the demand for imports—if the elasticity of demand for imports was greater than unity. With fewer foreign goods bought, there is a fall in foreign currency required to purchase those goods.

Any variation in these elasticities of demand will affect the net increase in foreign earnings, and it can be said that as long as the sum of the elasticity of demand for exports plus the elasticity of demand for imports is greater than unity, a devaluation of a currency is capable of bringing about a net increase in foreign earnings, i.e. the Marshall-Lerner condition. However, this is a necessary condition for a successful devaluation (or depreciation) of a currency, but there are quite a few other factors which may militate against the anticipated improvement in the balance of payments.

While the combined effect of the elasticities of demand for imports and exports is a crucial factor in the potential success of devaluation, an equally important complementary factor is the condition of supply of the country's exports and imports. There does not seem much point in the devaluation creating an excess demand for exports if the resources necessary for their production are not forthcoming. A full employment economy does not seem appropriate for this type of expenditure switching policy as import expenditure might well be moved to the home economy with possible inflationary overtones. Unless the government managed to deflate the economy and diverted goods from the home market, the essential supply of exported goods would not be able to satisfy the increased demand.

Foreign suppliers are frequently placed in a difficult position when they feel completely dependent on the UK market. The reduction in the goods they supply will obviously lower their income, and perhaps persuade them to reduce their domestic prices. By this action on the part of the foreign supplier, the volume of imports might still remain relatively high, resulting in a subsequent loss of foreign currency.

The devaluing country must take great care over the potential inflationary effect of the higher priced imports. The apparent inelasticity of demand of UK imports may well add to the cost push pressures within the economy. Trade unionists create further problems for themselves when they try to maintain their standard of living by claiming wage increases in excess of productivity. The full effect of this might well wipe out any of the cost advantages generated by the original devaluation and export earnings would not be so great.

Finally, devaluations can be self defeating if they contribute to retaliatory action by other countries. Competitive devaluations were not allowed within the Bretton Woods system of fixed exchange rates, and countries were expected to resort to devaluation only in attempts to remedy a fundamental disequilibrium.

Comment

A. Specific points

1. Division of the essay into **two** sections

   a. A relatively short introduction including definitions of the terms of trade and devaluation, showing that a devaluation will undoubtedly worsen the terms of trade.

   b. The major portion of the essay must include the many factors pertaining to the success of a devaluation, foremost among them being the state of the elasticities of demand for exports and imports.

2. Points of Emphasis

   a. The terms of trade: a key feature is the emphasis on *prices* and *not* on the total value of either exports or imports. The relative price movements of exports and imports are labelled adverse or favourable but this must not be confused necessarily with a deterioration or an improvement in the balance of trade.

   b. Devaluation: both depreciation and devaluation may well reflect a lower rate of exchange, but the former is the result of a downward movement within a floating exchange rate system, and the latter is a once and for all downward movement from one fixed parity to another fixed parity.

   c. Devaluation *must worsen* the terms of trade. It is how demand reacts to these price changes which will determine the *final values* of exports and imports. The relationship of these values will determine the net effect on the foreign currency involved.

   d. The Marshall-Lerner condition of elasticity of demand for exports and imports is the key factor in the potential success of a devaluation move.

   e. The elasticity of supply of both exports and imports can alter the prospective outcome of an alteration in the rate of exchange. The state of the economy in relation to full employment might entail a supplementary battery of deflationary controls so as to make room for the potential exports which the competitive edge of devaluation will give to its exporters. At the same time imported inflation must not be allowed to erode all the advantages gained by the lower exchange rate.

   f. Although devaluation does not by its nature automatically change the domestic home price of exports or the domestic foreign price of a country's imports, the devaluing country may well decide to raise its export prices in order to increase profits, while the foreign supplier might lower his price to maintain the sales of his goods. Both actions may well diminish the favourable influence which devaluation gave to a country's foreign earnings.

B. General points

1. Make sure that you understand the following terms

   a. elasticity of supply   **d.** adverse terms of trade
   b. devaluation   **e.** appreciation of sterling
   c. J curve effect   **f.** Marshall–Lerner theory.

2. Candidates find great difficulty in dealing with the following

   a. *The position of the terms of trade.*

   An understanding of this concept must fall back on a fundamental idea common throughout economics—opportunity cost. In a country, the opportunity cost of producing a unit of X is the quantity of Y which could be produced instead using the same resources. Trade will benefit both countries if the following conditions exist:

   i. The opportunity cost ratios of the countries are different.

   Example no. 1: Country A: 10X or 40Y Opportunity cost ratio: 1X = 4Y
                 Country B: 2X or 30Y Opportunity cost ratio: 1X = 15Y
   Example no. 2: Country A: 10X or 40Y Opportunity cost ratio: 1X = 4Y
                 Country B: 5X or 20Y Opportunity cost ratio: 1X = 4Y

   In both examples, country A has an absolute advantage over country B in both goods. In example number 1, country A has a *comparative* advantage in the production of good X while country B has a *comparative* advantage in the production of good Y. In example number 2, there is no *comparative* advantage for either country.

   ii. The terms of trade must fall somewhere between the two opportunity cost ratios: The terms of trade indicate the number of units of X which will exchange for a certain number of units of Y when trade takes place between countries A and B. The actual rate of exchange will be determined by the relative intensities of demand and supply for the products from the two countries.

   In example number 1 country A will not accept less than 4Y for 1X, while country B will not offer more than 15Y for 1X. Country A will concentrate on good X and country B will concentrate on good Y. If the terms of trade were 1X : 10Y *both* countries would gain from trading.

   If country B's demand for X was greater than country A's demand for Y what might the new rate of exchange become? (1X = 5Y *or* 1X = 14Y).

b. *The Marshall–Lerner Theory.*

One of the conditions for a successful devaluation is that the elasticities of demand for exports and imports must add up to more than unity.

Try to follow the story which is now given—

i. *Before Devaluation*: at a given exchange rate, £1 = $2.80, the UK exports 100 units of a good which has a domestic sterling price of £1 per unit, and at the same time imports 100 units of another good from the USA which has a domestic dollar price of $2.80 per unit. The UK will earn $280 from selling exports and spend $280 on imports.

ii. *Immediate Effect of Devaluation*: assumed that (1) sterling was devalued from £1 = $2.8 to £1 = $2.4, that is a 14.3% change and that (2) quantities of goods bought or sold remain unchanged, that is, a perfectly inelastic demand for exports and imports.

Exports: UK exports will have an unchanged domestic sterling price of £1 per unit but the dollar price will fall, i.e. to buy the 100 units Americans will only need $240. Each unit is now less expensive from the purchaser's point of view although the sterling price in the UK has not changed.

Imports: UK imports are supplied by foreigners and there will be an unchanged dollar price of $2.80 per unit, but the sterling price will rise, i.e. to buy the 100 units the British will require $280 but will have to pay more than £100 to obtain those dollars—in fact £116.66. Each unit is now more expensive from the purchasers' point of view, although the dollar price in America is unchanged. Under these circumstances the visible balance will move into deficit (−$40).

Intended Effect of Devaluation:

Devaluation is used as an emergency measure in order to improve the balance of payments. To be successful the measure must lead to a net increase in foreign currency earnings. Among the many factors determining its success or failure a crucial one is the relationship between the elasticity of demand for exports and imports.

(*a*) Elastic demand for exports: if demand rose by 30% the UK would sell 130 units at a sterling price of £1 per unit, and earn $312 from these exports.

(*b*) Inelastic demand for exports: if demand only rose by 5% the UK would sell 105 units at a sterling price of £1 per unit, and earn $252 from these exports.

(*c*) Elastic demand for imports: if demand for imports fell by 30% the UK would buy 70 units at a dollar price of $2.80 per unit, the imports costing $196 in foreign currency.

(*d*) Inelastic demand for imports: if demand for imports only fell by 5% the UK would buy 95 units at a dollar price of $2.80 per unit, the imports costing $266 in foreign currency.

Possible Combinations of Export and Import Demands.

i. Combination (*a*) and (*c*): the sum of the two elasticities is more than one.
$$(2.1 + 2.1 = 4.2)$$

ii. Combination (*b*) and (*d*): the sum of the two elasticities is less than one.
$$(0.35 + 0.35 = 0.70)$$

iii. Combination (*a*) and (*d*): the sum of the two elasticities is more than one.
$$(2.1 + 0.35 = 2.45)$$

iv. Combination (*b*) and (*c*): the sum of the two elasticities is more than one.
$$(0.35 + 2.1 = 2.45)$$

Which of the combinations will result in a surplus and which combinations will result in a deficit? Is the Marshall–Lerner condition upheld?

Essay questions

1. *Under what conditions, if any, is it reasonable for a country experiencing an import led inflation to devalue is currency?* (O/C Board)

2. *Distinguish between (a) 'terms of trade' and (b) 'balance of trade'. How is a country's balance of trade affected by changes in its terms of trade?* (IB)

3. *What are the probable consequences of devaluation for the country which devalues, on:*
   a. *the price level;*
   b. *the level of output;*
   c. *the Balance of Payments?* (Lond.)

4. *When, and for what reasons, might a government consider altering the exchange rate for the currency?* (O/C Board)

5. *How are the United Kindom's terms of trade measured? What effect will an adverse movement in the terms of trade have on the balance of payments?* (Oxf.)

Brief comments on essay questions

Question 2

The distinction between the two concepts in the title has proved, on many occasions, to be a stumbling block for many candidates. *Price, value* and *volume* are three interrelated terms which must be clearly appreciated in analysing 'the terms of trade' and 'the balance of trade'.

Suggested format for essay

Comparison:
a. Terms of trade—emphasis on *prices* and index numbers, making sure that the formula is correctly presented.
b. Balance of trade—this is the balance of visible trade within the context of the

current account of the balance of payments. Emphasis must be placed on the *value* aspect of this, which can only be obtained by combining the volume of goods traded with their respective prices. Clarify the point that invisible items are excluded from the balance of trade, which is itself only a part of the total balance of payments.

Effects of changes in terms of trade:
a. Briefly state how a change in the terms of trade may come about, e.g. devaluation, commodity boom.
b. Explain the term 'favourable' or 'adverse' in relation to the terms of trade.
c. Short term effects of deterioration in terms of trade: export prices fall relatively to import prices and assuming the volume of goods remain unchanged—in the short run—the balance of trade will deteriorate as well.
d. Longer-term effects of deterioration in terms of trade: elasticities of demand for imports and exports have had time to take effect on the volume of the goods, and so the value of goods traded may change. The balance of trade may improve or worsen after a change in the terms of trade.

Suggestions for further reading

Giles, C., ed. *Understanding Economics*. (The Manchester Economics Project—Ginn & Co. 1971.) Chapter 20

Lipsey, R. G. *An Introduction to Positive Economics*. (Weidenfeld & Nicolson, 1975.) Chapter 45

Harvey, J. *Modern Economics*. (Macmillan, 1971.) Chapter 33

Stanlake, G. F. *Macro-economics: An Introduction*. (Longman, 1975.) Chapter 18

Whitehead, G. *Economics Made Simple*. (W. H. Allen, 1974.) Chapter 23

Essay number 23

---

*Explain why the international monetary system of fixed but adjustable
exchange rates collapsed in 1973, and why countries adopted in its place
managed floating exchange rates.   (CA)*

Suggested answer

A specimen answer to this question will be given in *note form*, and the
following structure is suggested:

Introduction

(1) During the 18th and 19th centuries the international payments
system which gradually evolved became known as the gold standard.

(2) Its main features included domestic currencies being convertible into
gold, with exchange rates becoming fixed within certain limits. The loss of
gold from deficit countries necessitated the domestic economies being put
under pressure by deflationary policies which were supposed to bring
about a payments equilibrium.

What was the Adjustable Peg System?

(1) The Bretton Woods system encouraged international cooperation
by the member countries agreeing to maintain fixed parities within limits.

(2) The IMF supplied funds to help countries overcome temporary
payments' problems.

(3) Parities were to be adjusted in both directions to counteract a fundamental disequilibrium.

Important Point: the world was on a gold exchange standard as the
dollar was convertible into gold.

What were the problems facing this system?

(1) World liquidity consisted of gold, reserve currencies and withdrawal rights at the IMF. The expansion of world trade necessitated an increase in this liquidity which was not forthcoming from gold production, but was more than assisted by the surplus of dollars and sterling which the USA and UK thrust out into the world. The convertibility of the dollar was being seriously questioned by the fact that there was a diminishing supply of gold held at Fort Knox.

(2) The ability to adjust parities was rarely taken by countries, preference being given to demand management techniques. The protection of sterling throughout the post war period involved a maintenance of an overvalued rate by the technique of stop go policies.

(3) The gradual lack of confidence in the dollar and conversion into gold meant that other currencies found themselves in great difficulty trying to stop their exchange rates from appreciating (mark and yen). The economic difficulties within the USA, unemployment and high inflation, created serious balance of payments deficits which put the dollar under even more pressure.

Did the Smithsonian Agreement work?

(1) The 1971 Smithsonian agreement saw countries realigning their currencies with each other and maintaining parities within wider limits.

(2) USA succeeded in devaluing the dollar by raising the official price of gold to $38 per oz.

Important Point: suspension of dollar convertibility meant that the world was on a dollar standard.

The combination of the following events put severe pressure on the fixed rate system:

(a) the relative weakness of the United States economy with the consequent speculative effects on the dollar, coupled with world wide inflation.

(b) the arrival of the concept of the 'snake' created speculative pressure on various currencies.

(c) The increase in world commodity prices coupled with the OPEC oil price spiral created large dollar surpluses held by oil exporters which needed recycling throughout the depressed nations.

(d) the emergence of a Euro-dollar market allowed tremendous scope for short term capital movements which affected exchange rates throughout the world.

Conclusion

The present picture is of the IMF countries allowing their currencies to float, but making sure that the complex factors in the world would not

completely upset the steady trend a currency might attain by a system of
'dirty floating'.

Comments

A. Specific points

1. This essay is best divided into **two** sections of equal importance:

   a. An explanation of the pressures the Bretton Woods system faced;

   b. An explanation of the attempt to bring order to world exchange rates as seen in the Smithsonian Agreement.

2. Points of Emphasis

   a. Explanation of the adjustable peg system with its pattern of fixed exchange rates would include the requirements for a successful attainment of external equilibrium, namely sufficient reserves to maintain the rate of exchange, and a willingness for surplus countries to revalue or reflate, and deficit countries devaluing or deflating.

   b. The lynch pin of the entire gold exchange system was the confidence countries had in the ability of the USA to allow convertibility of the dollar into gold—itself based on the economic well being of the United States.

   c. The IMF system was crumbling at the seams because of a lack of world liquidity. Various schemes were initiated to solve this problem culminating in the attempt to introduce paper gold (special drawing rights).

   d. The pressure on the dollar became so great that the USA abandoned the convertibility of the dollar, thereby creating a dollar standard in effect. The realignment of currencies at the Smithsonian Conference 1971 was doomed to failure.

   e. The world reverted to a system of 'dirty floating' and attempts were made by the IMF to bring about an acceptable procedure in this case.

B. General points

1. Make sure you understand the following terms

a. gold specie points	**e.** special drawing rights
b. gold exchange standard	**f.** the snake
c. dollar standard	**g.** two tier gold price
d. currency swaps	**h.** dirty floating.

2. Candidates find great difficulty in appreciating the following ideas:

   a. *The Gold Standard*: there is no specific date when this system was initiated—it merely grew over time with countries being expected to obey the rules.

      i. A country's domestic currency was made convertible into gold at a price fixed by the country's authorities, which necessitated a strict control over the domestic money supply. Any difference in the gold and money supply would create problems for internal convertibility.

ii. The purchase and transfer of gold overseas meant that it became cheaper to redeem a debt in gold, sending it abroad, if the rate of exchange between two currencies ever reached certain limits. Thus the exchange rates between currencies became fixed within certain limits known as gold specie points.

iii. A country losing gold would be forced to reduce the money supply by deflationary action. If the action reacted on the domestic employment and price levels, external equilibrium would result as exports responded to the lower prices.

iv. The problems facing the gold standard in the 1920s, such as countries with unrealistic parities, a world depression, rigid price and wage levels etc., necessitated action from some countries which tended to destroy the smooth working of such a system. Countries protected themselves from the ravages of unemployment and recession by the use of tariff barriers and competitive devaluations. The end result was a fall in the volume of world trade with no country benefiting.

b. *The Gold Exchange Standard*: the system envisaged by the Bretton Woods Conference of 1944 required a powerful American economy. The soundness of the USA economy and its currency, the dollar, remained the key to the whole system. Foreign monetary authorities were allowed to convert dollars into gold at the official price of gold, but the importance of the dollar meant that countries were quite prepared to hold a fund of reserve currencies (dollars and sterling) in their central banks in the secure knowledge that they could be converted into gold quite easily. The amount of gold held in the Federal Reserve Bank and the confidence placed in the dollar determined the success of the international payments system!

c. *The Liquidity Problem*: a system dependent on maintaining exchange rates at certain parities required an ample supply of foreign exchange. Internationally acceptable money consisted of gold, reserve currencies and borrowing rights at the IMF. This total of foreign exchange had to cope with an expansion in world trade and inflationary upheavals. The cost of producing gold was on the increase but the official price of gold in the early 1960s was still at $35 per oz. The supply of gold became extremely limited to demand, and with private and industrial demand for gold growing, there was less available for monetary purposes. There was still an ever increasing quantity of liquidity being generated by the USA and the UK in the form of reserve currencies, but these were now being placed under some pressure by the relative position of their balance of payments. The convertibility of dollars into gold by certain foreign countries—France and Germany—meant a significant decrease in America's gold reserves.

d. *The Adjustment Problem*: whatever exchange rate a country decides to maintain, it becomes obvious that, over time, growth rates and inflationary rates will change. This will mean that one is trying to maintain a rate which is no longer valid and relevant to the changed circumstances. New circumstances demand a new rate of exchange but reasons abound why countries were loath to do so:

i. Would it be a potential success? Were all the circumstances in its favour?
ii. A reserve currency country would have to consider the undoubted repercussions on a great number of countries.
iii. A country dependent on its invisible earnings might consider that confidence in its currency demanded no change in the rate of exchange.
iv. The alternative to lowering the exchange rate might be deflationary action, but countries like the UK avoided savage deflationary measures as it tended to have more influence on unemployment than on prices.

e. *The Dollar Standard*: In 1968 there were two prices of gold—an official price and a free market price. Pressure on the dollar had reached such a stage of concern that in 1971 the USA's obligation to convert dollars into gold at the official price was brought to an end. Countries continued to hold dollars in their reserves but it was not convertible into gold. The dollar was dependent on a strong USA economy. The gold held by central banks in their reserves was more or less frozen as long as the free market price was above the official price. Agreement was reached to attempt the gradual run down of the use of gold as a monetary unit, and with the IMF selling off gold by auction, the likely outcome is the demonetisation of gold.

f. *Current Picture of the Exchange Rate System—a world of 'dirty' floating*: The picture is extremely complex and can change at any time, but in early 1978 the pattern was as follows:
　There were 3 main groups of countries
i. Countries centred round the German mark (the snake)—floating
ii. Countries centred round the American dollar—floating
iii. Another group including the UK and France—floating.

The snake: it was born in 1972 containing most of the EEC countries. The member countries agreed to limit movements in cross-parities to $2\frac{1}{4}$% either side of the central rates fixed between any two European countries, while making sure that movements against the dollar were also to be limited to an overall fluctuation of $4\frac{1}{2}$% (a tunnel).

In 1973 the snake was allowed to float against the dollar, and the tunnel was abandoned. Sterling had left the snake prior to this date. If the snake countries see an undue appreciation of one of their currencies action must be taken by *both* countries. If the German mark is in great demand compared with the Dutch guilder both countries must buy guilders in the foreign exchange market. The monetary authorities of both countries must intervene with Holland even having to borrow marks from the German Central Bank for the purpose. An array of countries have been associated with the snake, staying inside until their currency apparently came under too much pressure. In early 1978 the snake comprised West Germany, Denmark, Norway, Belgium, Netherlands and Luxemburg.

Figure 1 will give an approximate indication of how the rates of exchange of rival currencies have altered since the Smithsonian Agreement of 1971.

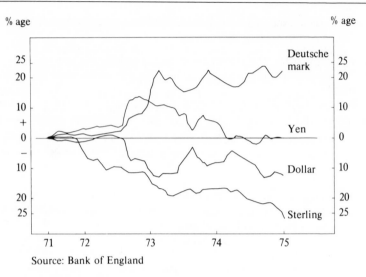

Source: Bank of England

Fig. 1   Percentage change of major currencies since Smithsonian Agreement (Dec 21st 1971)

The complexity of the exchange rate system can be simplified by categorising currencies as follows:

Currencies floating independently: 11 (UK, Canada, Japan, Switzerland, etc.)
Currencies floating jointly: 7 (the snake)
Currencies pegged to a single currency: 81 (54 of whom pegged to the $)
Currencies pegged to a composite basket of currencies: 19

The independent floaters and joint floaters cover 70% of the value of IMF members' trade.

Essay questions

     1. *What is meant by world liquidity? How can it be increased?*   *(IB)*

     2. *Describe the events since 1970 culminating in the breakdown of the post war system of fixed exchange rates.*   *(IB)*

     3. *What is the International Monetary Fund? Does it deal satisfactorily with the problem of international liquidity?*   *(Lond.)*

     4. *Analyse the relative advantages and disadvantages of floating and fixed exchange rates, making use in your answer of the United Kingdom's experience of a floating exchange rate in recent years.*   *(Oxf.)*

     5. *Estimate the effect of special drawing rights on the development of international trade.*   *(AEB)*

Brief comments on essay questions

Question 3

Although this question is divided conveniently into *two* parts, it is the assessment of the effectiveness of the IMF which will prove most difficult for many candidates.

The first section requires the presentation of the main principles upon which the IMF works, and an explanation of such principles.

a. A fixed exchange rate system but with an adjustable peg proviso.

b. A quota system enabling a pool of gold and foreign currencies to assist debtor nations.

c. Maintenance of a specific par value (within limits) for a country's currency.

d. Scarce currency clause to deal with countries experiencing persistent surpluses.

The second section enables the better candidate to exhibit his understanding of the post-war experiences. This can be dealt with by allocating time to the following periods:

a. 1945–1960s—reasonable success.

b. 1960s–1971—IMF challenged by problems of inadequate liquidity, adjustment problems, lack of confidence in the USA.

c. 1971 onwards—the Smithsonian Agreement and the final development of 'dirty floating'.

Suggestions for further reading

Lipsey, R. G. *An Introduction to Positive Economics*. (Weidenfeld & Nicolson, 1975.) Chapter 47

Livesey, F. *A Textbook of Economics* (Polytech Publishers Ltd, 1978.) Chapter 15

Stanlake, G. F. *Introductory Economics* (Longman, 1971.) Chapters 28–29